Like all objects in motion in our universe, the laws of physics apply to price movement. Trajectory Forex uses real time data to consistently identify winning trends with a scientific method never before used in forex or any other trading marketplace.

\

TRAJECTORY FOREX
By J. A. Sparks
First Edition
Published by WhitakerSparks
© Copyright 2011 by J. A. Sparks
All rights reserved.
ISBN 978-0-615-44770-4

The author hereby grants all purchasers of this book permission to download and view, at no additional cost, all charts used as examples of trading activity in this book by visiting: www.TrajectoryForex.com.

For permission to access or reproduce any other content, please contact: trajectoryforex@gmail.com

WHITAKER SPARKS
A Virginia Publishing Company

Trajectory Forex

Contents

Introduction

The Trajectory Forex methodology might, on some levels, seem relatively simple. There's a reason. The system is indeed pretty basic both in concept and execution, even though there is a somewhat complex mathematical foundation behind the entire analytical process. Compared to the complexity, complication and predictive flaw of traditional Technical Analysis, Trajectory Forex trend identification is an innovative, fact-based revolution.

The key to your success with Trajectory Forex will be attention to detail in executing each step as explained, and patience through the initial learning process. There is an element of judgment, but it is neither monumentally difficult nor does it require significant math skills. Trajectory Forex simply involves observation of two pieces of 100% true, real time quantitative data that stream live into your MT4 trading platform, and then analyzing this data to make qualitative trading decisions.

The important thing to remember is that the system works if you diligently follow the discipline outlined here. I've been implementing this system successfully since 2006, which means it has proven to be consistently profitable both in strong and unstable global financial conditions.

A few weeks prior to this writing, a fellow who had been practicing Trajectory trend identification for about a month opened a $3000 cash account with a forex broker. In his first two days of trading, he made a $1780 net profit. So, after 48 hours, he had account equity of $4780, which means more trades and potentially higher profits. In this sense, account growth in forex is exponential; not incremental as in other trading marketplaces. You'll see more examples of the consistent profits produced by Trajectory Forex on subsequent pages.

While most brokers allow you to open an account with deposits as small as $300, it can take 10 to 14 days to double such a small amount. Of course, with the high leverage in forex (50 to 1 and up to 500 to 1), account growth then becomes increasingly rapid with each increase in total equity.

In forex, perhaps more than any other marketplace, the size of your account is the biggest variable that determines the level of profits you can earn. Small account traders must build up their account equity more slowly in order to achieve higher levels of profit. Available margin, or the total dollars in your account, is critical to the size and number of trades you can make and this directly impacts your total profitability.

I can't promise you will get any specific measure of profitable results, but I can offer that the average trader using Trajectory Forex since 2007 has earned $1600 to $4000 every 24 hours. No doubt, results vary from one trader to the next, and there is no guarantee you will make any profit at all. Past performance does not equal future results.

As you will read later in this book, I'm not an advocate of predicting the future of anything in the universe, and that includes financial trading. All we have in life and finance are statistical probabilities. So, in addition to reminding you to read the long disclaimer at the end of this book, I'll offer that the past performance of Trajectory Forex traders allows me to suggest only that there is a reasonable probability you will succeed.

I have been teaching people to trade with the Trajectory Forex methodology since 2007. So far, not one trader has told me it fails to work. Everyone's results vary, however, depending on their individual skill in execution. I have also had students simply quit because they become impatient and frustrated. We'll discuss the psychology required to be successful in trading later in this text. Bottom line, the Trajectory methodology works. The biggest variable is you.

Equally noteworthy, this methodology for trend identification works in other markets beyond Forex. Trajectory can be used to trade stocks on the New York Stock Exchange or NASDAQ, for example. Anywhere you have a commodity with a price that fluctuates over a period of extended time, and these price fluctuations can be monitored accurately in real time, then this method will work to help you identify profit taking trend opportunities.

As a quick overview of how and why this system works, I'll offer a brief metaphor that spares you from the laws of physics at play in Trajectory Forex.

Imagine that you're sitting on top of a mountain about a mile high above a valley. Down in the valley, through your binoculars, you can see two cars moving north and south. The only information you can evaluate relative to the movement of each car is every individual mile traveled, and the time it takes for each car to move one mile after another. So, as you observe the two cars moving north and south in the valley, you wake up one morning and see that the RED car has moved north 20 miles in just 30 minutes. On that same day, you see that the BLUE car has moved south for the same distance of 20 miles, BUT it took 18 hours to travel the distance. You also note that the RED car has been moving the same northern direction fairly consistently at a good speed for several days, while the BLUE car has been going north, then south, then north...changing direction each day.

Now, as you sit on your mountaintop with only these two pieces of information (total miles traveled and the time it took for each of the RED and BLUE cars to travel those north and south distances), which car in the above example is more statistically probable to continue going in the same direction?

I hope the answer is obvious.

The RED car that's traveled 20 miles in 30 minutes clearly has established speed and thus momentum. Something is causing this car to move north over a longer period of time with strong velocity. The causal effect prompting the consistent northern direction of movement might be the driver's desire to go north to visit the bank or to see his wife. It doesn't matter. What we know by mere observation of the quantitative trajectory with velocity is that the RED car has a higher qualitative statistical probability of continued movement in the same northern direction. We don't need to know the reason why. It's just happening.

The BLUE car that's traveled south the same 20 miles, but took 18 hours to go that distance and seems to have no pattern of consistent directional movement is more likely to retrace, reverse, or just stop and go sideways. There's no strong velocity driving the BLUE car north or south, and thus little momentum. There appears to be no causal effect fueling a consistent trajectory of movement either north or south. By mere observation of this quantitative trajectory weakness, we know there is a low qualitative statistical probability of any consistent or continued movement in one or the other direction.

The comparison above expresses the general concept behind Trajectory analysis. More is explained in detail later, of course. The methodology, however, is fundamentally based on calculating the trajectory of a moving object, whether it is real or virtual (i.e. automobiles or currency prices). We are applying basic principles of physics to the real time motion of a virtual object that exists in our universe. Does this make sense?

Do you see how "price" can be looked at as a virtual object with a trajectory (just like a physical object in motion), and we can accurately measure the trajectory at any point in time given the proper information in terms of direction of motion and velocity?

You'll find the system works consistently in terms of mathematics because, in forex and other markets, we actually do get real time price movement data plus the time frames of each movement. So, we have direction of motion and velocity! This allows us to calculate statistical probabilities for ongoing directional movement of our virtual object in motion (currency price) based on the physics that apply to every object in our known universe.

In forex, the essential data streams into your MT4 trading platform 24 hours a day, 6 days a week and is perhaps the most easily accessed information available to consumers in any financial market. Your challenge now is merely learning the art and science of analyzing this data.

This is where you will most likely make mistakes in the early stages of trading. One of the biggest problems we must all overcome is the tendency to look at data and repeatedly try to see what we want to see versus the objective reality of the numbers.

There are simply more times when there is no trend than genuine opportunities to make profits. When you get close to seeing a trend via this methodology, it is truly difficult to hold your breath and keep your finger from hitting buy or sell on your computer. We all want to make money. So, the discipline to avoid taking chances on a "possible" trend you think you've spotted is the biggest challenge you will confront on a repeated basis.

Even after several years of successful Trajectory Forex trading, I still catch myself prematurely jumping onto a trend that suddenly retraces or reverses, and will either become a prolonged sideways movement or a legitimate, potentially costly reverse. Mistakes happen! That's part of statistical probability, which is central to this trend identification system. Your ability to quickly acknowledge a mistake or unanticipated fluctuation will be central to your long-term success.

You can also think of this like golf. If you hit a few shots into the rough, it's okay as long as you smartly hit the next shot onto the green. Not even the best professional golfers hit every shot perfectly. The legends of the game are those who recover smartly from their mistakes, and manage to avoid repeatedly hitting the ball into one hazard after another. You won't make the cut if you repeatedly make big mistakes. Control is key. Determination is essential. The ability to recover from occasional mistakes is mandatory. This is golf. This is life. This is forex.

Overall, I submit that this process of calculating statistical probabilities is the strongest possible methodology you can use to trade forex or any other market. If there were such things as statistical absolutes or consistently accurate signals in trading, you'd have millionaires on every street corner.

So, the real question becomes how skillful you can make yourself at identifying stronger and stronger statistical "probabilities". This also tests your level of risk tolerance.

For an impatient trader or one with too high a risk tolerance, failure and financial losses are almost predestined. I strongly urge those wishing to make a quick buck or get rich quick to try something else besides investing in forex, or stocks, or any other market.

No doubt, with the leverage in forex, traders can make a lot of money in a very short time. The problem with aiming for quick riches in short periods of time is the inherent risk in trying to "force" good fortune, and likely trying to ride out retraces which can quickly become fatally costly. In forex, profits grow exponentially but so do losses. You can totally destroy an account with a few bad trades that get out of control in the pursuit of fast money.

Patience. Diligent hard work. Analysis of data. Accepting small losses, while capturing reasonable, but the largest possible profits on winning trades. These are all characteristics that are mandatory if you are to achieve success. You cannot wish or hope a trend into existence. You cannot wish or hope a trend will continue just because it's manifested itself for a period of time as you anticipated. All trends come to an end. The market will give you trends and it will take them away. This is reality. All a trader can do is evaluate real time data and make decisions as to statistical probability relative to the market's behavior.

If you can live with this measure of patience and diligent, intense hard work, then you can succeed at trading literally anything in a financial market. If you are looking for a magic solution or instant riches, you are better off buying a lottery ticket.

SPECIAL NOTE ON GRAPHICS: You will note resolution of some charts and graphs may not be of the highest quality as they appear later in this book. This is because I was capturing these screen shots on the go while also trading forex. If you wish to see higher quality images plus additional content related to Trajectory Forex trading, please visit: www.TrajectoryForex.com. You can download higher resolution images of everything pictured in this book at no cost at that website.

1

Trade In The Now

The most important thing to remember when trading with the Trajectory Forex methodology is to make decisions based on real time data. One way to keep this top of mind is a simple phrase I repeat to myself still today when watching forex charts and making trades: Trade In The Now.

This should become your mantra. It should be playing in your mind non-stop as you look at charts and evaluate the statistical probabilities that identify a trend. Trade In The Now, and you will profit. Trade In The Now, and you will forever suffer only small losses. Trade In The Now, and you will always have the confidence to maximize your profits.

Trade In The Now. Remember that phrase. It creates wealth.

A trend that happened three days ago only has value as it relates to real time price movement now. So, while we definitely want to take into consideration the price movement behavior of multiple time frames, including recent and increasingly distant past price movements, we primarily focus on what's happening now within that context. Are you going to make money because of what happened to price movement an hour ago? Yesterday? The past six months?

No.

You will make money only on what is going to happen to price movement in the next few seconds, minutes and hours that are about to happen. Equally significant, you cannot predict the future. So guessing, or attempting to predict the future is futile.

This is the core flaw of Technical Analysis, perhaps the most common and popular technique for trading forex today. It is fatally flawed and the reason no less than 80% of all new traders who first get into forex lose all their money.

The lethal combination of chart patterns and indicators in Technical Analysis are set up to identify profit opportunities based on PAST price performance. Unfortunately, history does not repeat itself, especially not to the high degree of accuracy one needs in order to risk actual money and make profits consistently.

Just because a certain formation of price movements seen in the past has "usually" indicated price movement in one or the other direction, that same formation of recent price fluctuations (usually candle patterns in forex charts) does NOT destine the same price movement behavior in the future. Again, history does not repeat itself.

Technical Analysis is thus fatally flawed because it is predictive in nature. As we learned in grade school, you cannot predict the future. It is a law of the universe, and that includes investing.

The probabilities that are calculated with historical technical data are not remotely reliable as those calculated with 100% true real time data. This is the difference between Trajectory data-based trend identification and Technical Analysis. There is no predicting in Trajectory Forex. The data used to determine statistical probabilities in Trajectory Forex is 100% true, and streams non-stop to your computer in real time. So you are constantly making decisions in the now. You are trading in the now...not based on the past.

If you have previously learned Technical Analysis, I advise you to try and forget it entirely. Price resistance levels, channels, spinning tops, psychological and historical price barriers...none of these elements in Technical Analysis have meaning relative to price movement today. There are no rules to supply and demand. There are no repeat patterns you can rely upon in price movement. There is only data. There is only empirical reality as it happens, and the undeniable, factual statistical probabilities that are constantly present in all conditions if you are capable of calculating them.

You must approach trading as if you are a scientist calculating the physics of a moving object in space. You must base all decisions on data, and data alone.

Now, I will be the first to admit that some traders who have learned Trajectory Forex apply it in concert with Technical Analysis. I don't dispute the success they report to me at times. This is a matter of personal choice. I simply advise that Technical Analysis seeks to predict the future, which is impossible in our known universe. So, I suggest that you abandon this voodoo. But, it is your choice.

Not surprisingly, I also urge traders to forget everything they know about Fundamental Analysis. It is also flawed and fails the test of consistent success long term. Interpretation of real world events is highly subjective. It challenges one to take into consideration every possible element of influence. Do you "really" know all the information that impacts a news announcement? Are you ahead of the reaction to this news, or behind it? How do you know?

Fundamental Analysis, or evaluation of trading opportunities based on interpretation of the impact of real world events, is also flawed. No one is privy to all the information. Worse, it is impossible for the consumer trader to take into consideration every global event in perfect, harmonious synergy. Yes. A news announcement about high unemployment may have a strong impact on the value of the U.S. Dollar (USD). But, does this mean the USD will go up or down in relation to the Euro (EUR) when there are also riots in the streets of France because of government instability? Does news about the Chinese refusing to purchase U.S. debt have more impact than positive economic growth in America? It's a fundamental guessing game, not a methodology that helps assure consistent, trustworthy success in identification of trends.

These myriad real world factors are almost impossible to pull into one set of calculations and come out with a trustworthy anticipation of price movement. At least I will offer that it's just about impossible for the average consumer trader to achieve such knowledge.

In Forex, I strongly urge traders to forget Technical and Fundamental Analysis. If we allow ourselves to even think about such considerations, we can skew our objective analysis of data in the Trajectory Forex methodology.

Free your mind. Turn off the news. Don't look at current events on the web. The real time data in your forex trading platform will tell you all you need to know about what is happening in the world outside. The less you know, the less your subjective opinion will influence what must be data-based decisions on the Trajectory of price movement.

In this sense, ignorance is bliss in forex. You do NOT want to think about subjective, interpretive or predictive things. You want to exclusively Trade In The Now and base all decisions on 100% true data. Trade on data alone.

In Trajectory Forex, this means trading ONLY based on two variables: price movement and time frames. The only two pieces of information we have in Forex, or any other market, that are 100% true at all times are actual price movement as we see in real time and the time frames for price movement.

In other words, if a price has moved up 10 pips (or points), did it move 10 pips up in 5 minutes on the heels of an overall move of 100 pips in the same direction over the prior two hours? Or did it take six hours to move 10 pips upwards with multiple swings up and down over the prior 24 hours? Big difference. One is a trend. The other is a trap. One has a high probability of continued movement and thus presents a profit opportunity. The other is a likely trap just inviting you to lose money.

So let's say you see the rapid, strong upward price movement exactly as described above in the short time frame (indicating faster movement and thus momentum). You then place a buy order, and your money is in play. But, let's say that seconds after placing this intelligent trade, there is hesitation in price movement. It goes sideways for a full 60 seconds. Then, unexpectedly, the price moves 6 pips downward over the next five minutes. What do you do given all that prior price movement upwards? By every element of trajectory, it "looked" like a trend that should continue!

We strongly recommend you implement a simple money management technique. I will call this the "Max Loss Rule". This is the maximum amount of money you are willing or able to lose on any given trade. The number of pips worth of movement you wait to see if your trend returns to the previously identified direction is your Max Loss Limit. So, if you can only afford a loss of 10 pips, then you are okay if just a 6 pip retrace transpires. You can continue to watch the price movement and see if it resumes the upward momentum that is so statistically probable to continue. If, however, you can only afford a 5 pip loss, then you should instantly close out your trade. Take the small loss and abide by your Max Loss Rule.

Then, however, don't just walk away in defeat. Stay at your computer after suffering the small loss and see what happens. In most cases, like the one described above, all you are seeing is a slight correction or price retrace, and the trend will resume. When it takes off upwards again, simply Trade In The Now and make yet another buy trade.

If statistical probabilities based on real time data hold true, then you "should" collect profits that outweigh your losses from the prior trade. If not, you get out again if your max loss limit is hit. Then you seriously have to watch this price movement, because what has happened?

If you have suffered two small losses, then your trend has likely ended. You can continue watching. Two losses is not a rule. There are no "rules". The trend might take off again and, with immense diligence and patience, I would jump right back into that trade with yet another buy. (I would wait to see more than a few pips worth of movement in the original trend direction, but I would not hesitate to trust the data that I'm seeing "if" the trend resumes.)

Bottom line, you are always Trading In The Now. You are always aware that things can change in an instant. But, you must trust statistical probabilities. The above example is likely remote. If you see as much movement in one direction as I detailed above, you are not likely going to enter your trade at the exact moment the price retraces substantially on you. Nor is the price movement likely to resume, encourage you to enter yet another trade, but then suddenly retrace a second time. The statistical probabilities of this happening are pretty remote based on the strong movement described above. But, it could happen. That's why we have Max Loss Rules. That's why we Trade In The Now.

If you are like me, and you make a mistake that costs you money, you'll likely find it was just plain sloppy analysis. You moved too soon. You selectively dismissed price movement velocity as seen in one or two important time frames because it didn't fit what you "wanted" to see. Or, you simply misread price movement velocity in the time frame charts.

There is a lot of wishful thinking in all of us. Sometimes, we will look at data and see only what we want to see. Avoid that mistake. Always trust the data. This is another reason to do extensive demo trading to establish your own pattern of objective analytical processes and build your confidence in every trading decision.

But if a currency moves against you and goes beyond your maximum loss number, get out of that trade with only a small loss. If the trend continues as you identified in the real time data, ride that trend for as much profit as you can capture. Then, inevitably, when you see a problematic retrace, get out. Always remember that trends come to an end. Don't be stubborn. Be practical.

Also acknowledge that you can't win every single trade. Even after years of profitable trading, you will look at data, identify a trend, and it will disappear before your eyes. This is just the nature of price movement in every financial market in the world. It cannot be predicted. Statistically remote things happen every day. Fortunately for us, statistically probable things hold true more routinely, and that's why you should make profits on a consistent basis.

When approaching forex with this systematic, patient, diligent, data-based system, you should inevitably win profits. Consistently winning trades is the end result of physics applied to forex just as it is applied to every other system in our known universe. You can't predict the future of any system with 100% accuracy, but you can identify statistically probable trends. This is how we profit in trade after trade.

So, with Trajectory techniques, you will have successful trading days. You may likely have streaks of a couple weeks where you win profits on just about every trade. It's going to happen. You are going to get pretty good at looking at the data, and trading profitably based on statistical probabilities. But, don't let confidence become a costly enemy.

I'm sure you've heard the phrase, "Past performance does not equal future results." That is a phrase we must remember every minute we trade in our real time data-based world. You must always trade in the now, even if it means you must accept a small loss and acknowledge a mistake on the heels of several weeks of success. Trust the data you see right now before your eyes. Never fall victim to the belief that you will be right today because you were right the past twenty days.

Your own past success is not an indicator of future success on any next day ahead. Emotions are a huge threat to your success in trading forex or any other market. Overconfidence is just as much a concern as fear of failure.

A lot of people I've mentored in Trajectory Forex enjoy big success over the first couple weeks. Then, they often become reckless.

They will start to "hope" a currency will return to the trend they were so confident was real and strong. Yes, you can trust the data. But you must also realize this is all happening in real time and things can change dramatically in seconds. This is especially true in today's world where a single government intervention to temporarily prop up a currency's value in forex can cause everything to change against all odds and everything you saw in terms of analysis.

The price movement trajectory you calculated and earned profits from over the past two weeks is not destined to continue indefinitely. Realizing the signs of that possible end to the trend is critical. So always Trade In The Now! Trust the data you see now to make decisions and never rely on yesterday's success as a false indicator of confidence in a shaky trend today.

Limit your losses according to your Max Loss Rule if something goes wrong.

None of us can predict the future. All we have in heaven and earth are statistical probabilities based on real time data.

Suffering a small loss and coming back the next hour to make that money back is a good thing. It's an easy thing. Suffering some huge loss because you got emotional and were stubborn about how you "read" the data is just foolish and can be very costly. Be smart. Be patient. Be aware that things can change.

They key to success is to avoid making that one big mistake. It does no good for you to win 100 trades, earn profits on each of those smartly won trades, but then turn around and make one huge mistake in one bad trade that costs you a fortune. It's like driving a car in the city. You can go through 100 traffic intersections intelligently, safely, and always watching the signals. You can also get instantly killed if you ignore a single signal, run one red light, and get smashed by a giant truck.

So win consistently. Win as big as possible on every correctly identified trade. But, if and when you inevitably make a losing decision, lose small. Slam on your brakes at the sudden appearance of an oncoming truck and avoid a fatal accident.

This is the key to long term profitability and ultimate riches whether they happen in a couple weeks, a couple months, or years. It's also how you keep that wealth versus getting emotional and going on the crazy up and down streaks I also hear about from forex investors.

Always stay positive. Always focus on the data. Learn to enjoy trading, and start having fun. That's when you should make more profits than you ever imagined.

2

Beyond Multiple Time
Frame Analysis

I want to write a brief chapter early in this book to make sure you comprehend the fact that Trajectory Forex is NOT simply a re-packaged version of Multiple Time Frame Analysis (MTFA).

MTFA was introduced a few decades ago and quickly absorbed into Technical Analysis. Still, as I have introduced my Trajectory methodology to veteran traders, I repeatedly have to respond to a question they often ask after taking an initial look at Trajectory Forex. This is NOT simply MTFA with a different name.

Multiple Time Frame Analysis (MTFA) suggests you look at the same "windows" to data, if you will, but it does not remotely attempt to access or analyze the same nature or depth of data we use in Trajectory trend identification.

MTFA is a methodology I would compare to people looking at a forest, but they cannot see the trees. The level of detail, depth of data observed, and nature of data analysis is both different and signifi-cantly more comprehensive in Trajectory.

For example, MTFA analysts routinely suggest that you simply pick two or three time frames and merely look for alignment to make a trading decision (typically in concert with other Technical indicators, which we know to be factually unreliable). So, an MTFA trading decision might be based on looking at the Daily chart to see an up or down trend, and then confirming that you have the same direction of trend movement in a shorter time frame, like H1 or M30. If you see alignment of the same direction of movement, then MTFA suggests that this is all you need to know to make a trade.

Unfortunately, this is reckless and insufficient in terms of data analysis. MTFA completely ignores the second key variable in Trajectory Forex, velocity. Thus, MTFA will routinely be brutally misleading. There is much more to the analysis of price movement trajectory than mere alignment. This is one reason MTFA has never really earned a place alongside Technical or Fundamental Analysis as a legitimate trend identification methodology. It's simply been wrapped into Technical Analysis as "one" of the many indicators a trader can use to make decisions. It does not stand on its own as Trajectory does in terms of consistently reliable trend identification.

As well, most MTFA traders with whom I've talked routinely disregard what they call "noise". They discount the M1, M5 and even M15 time frames because they show only minor retraces of no significance in conventional MTFA. So, most MTFA traders will take the longer term trends and trust them to make trading decisions.

This is perilous and invites losing trades, because (as you will see on subsequent pages) the shorter time frames such as M1 and M5 are critical first indicators of a change in the velocity of a price trajectory. If we ignore velocity as a real time data variable, then we might as well toss physics out the window. Velocity is critical to charting the trajectory of an object in motion (physical or virtual).

While MTFA only looks for alignment in a couple of different time frame charts, Trajectory Forex looks for alignment and velocity in the comprehensive range of time frames.

We view the currency price as if it is a virtual object moving through space. We are using the real time data to calculate its trajectory just as we would calculate the trajectory of a jet plane or any other object in motion. Then, we are making a determination as to the statistical probability for continued momentum in the same direction based on our observation of the overall and relative velocity of movement.

This is not mere alignment (not just a couple snapshots of an object in motion as seen in different time frames), which is the stated goal of conventional MTFA. Mere alignment of a few or even all time frames does NOT identify a true and sustained trajectory of price or any object in motion. For example, you might have a very slow moving price with a very weak velocity...little to no momentum. Yet, every single time frame might align perfectly in the same direction to produce a magnificent deception.

In other words, if you were using Multiple Time Frame Analysis to evaluate the trending of an automobile, you might see that it has been moving north for the past several hours, and it has continued to move north over the past 15 minutes. This, according to basic MTFA teaching, is enough for you to consider making a trade to earn pips on continued north movement of the car.

With Trajectory, we will not only look at the north movement of that same car, but we will determine how many pips per hour the car has been moving. We will perhaps see that the car has been moving about 20 net pips per hour north over the past 10 days. It has continued to move north at about 15 net pips per hour over the past several hours, and it has maintained this direction and speed over the past 15 to 30 minutes. As well, we will look at minute by minute movement, and further confirm that the car continues to move north at about 20 to 15 net pips per hour with only very minor fluctuations in that speed in real time.

Trajectory takes analysis of data to a much higher level than MTFA. In Trajectory, we are calculating not only direction of movement, but also velocity of movement. This allows us, as with the above north moving car, to determine the statistical probability of continued movement north. In the above example, we can be confident the north movement of the car will continue because of the sustained high speed and subsequent momentum derived from this ongoing velocity.

At the same time, Trajectory allows us to use the M1 and M5

short term time frames to watch for any changes in the speed of our moving car. When we suddenly see the speed of movement drop for a few minutes to 1 mile per hour and then it goes into reverse, we watch carefully to see if the reverse or stalled movement continues in the M5 time frame. In MTFA, these short time frame movements are disregarded and commonly referred to as "noise". In Trajectory, we carefully evaluate velocity of movement and sustained momentum in order to be very quick to identify potential major change of direction. Again, Trajectory far surpasses MTFA as a data analysis methodology.

From another metaphorical perspective, MTFA traders seek to identify trends by looking at a few snapshot photos of an object in motion in order to determine direction. Trajectory traders evaluate real time price movement by looking at what is effectively a live video feed of data over extended periods of time in order to see not only the direction of movement but also the consistent or varied speed of the object as it has been and continues moving.

Now, I do not claim to be an MTFA expert and explaining MTFA is not the purpose of this book. So if you are a big believer in MTFA, please keep that in mind and do not take offense at my somewhat superficial overview of that methodology. Still, my experience has been that Trajectory is a more in-depth and analytical approach to the accurate measurement of an object's movement in space and time. Trajectory Forex allows us to not only see directional alignment, but also identify velocity, evaluate its strength, and thus calculate the probability of continued directional momentum.

Our confidence that momentum will continue is based on the knowledge that movement is not random. It is the result of some causal effect. This is why alignment of direction is not enough information to make a trade. We must evaluate speed of movement in a certain direction, and this allows us to conclude probability that a strong causal effect is present and will thus continue to motivate same direction of movement. So, it's not "just" momentum. It is continued movement based on momentum that results from some driving force (some fundamental economic set of variables we don't need to identify, but simply be aware of relative to the effect on our moving object.)

I apologize for jumping in a bit deep at this early point in the book. All I really want to establish for you at this stage is that the Trajectory methodology for trend identification is legitimately unique and in no way as simplistic as Multiple Time Frame Analysis. MTFA is a superficial point of view that does not even come close to the level of data analysis we conduct in Trajectory.

Again, MTFA does indeed put you in front of the correct tele-scope to see the desired movement of an object in space. But, it does not teach, encompass nor embrace the calculations of data necessary to determine actual and sustained or changing velocity, directional certainty, and legitimate statistical probability of continued move-ment of that object you see out there in the universe.

Trajectory Forex is a significant evolution several generations beyond MTFA. Do NOT assume you can merely trade based on alignment. It's a mistake. We're going to determine trends based on a much higher level of data analysis, so sharpen your pencil. We're not just looking for same direction of movement in a couple of different time frames.

Trajectory analysis is a significant advance over any trend identification methodology ever seen in forex or any other trading marketplace.

TRAJECTORY FOREX WORKS. PERIOD.

2011.02.02 14:06	0.93363	-9.52	9 245.63
2011.02.02 14:06	0.93364	-9.52	9 236.96
2011.02.02 14:07	0.93402	-9.52	8 899.17
2011.02.02 14:07	0.93400	-9.52	8 916.49
2011.02.02 14:07	0.93406	-9.52	8 873.09
2011.02.02 14:07	0.93406	-9.52	8 864.53
2011.02.02 14:07	0.93429	-9.52	8 665.40
2011.02.02 14:07	0.93424	-9.52	8 700.12
2011.02.02 14:07	0.93438	-9.52	8 570.39

2011.02.02 14:08	0.93435	-9.52	8 527.85
2011.02.02 14:08	0.93432	-9.52	8 553.81
2011.02.02 14:08	0.93435	-9.52	8 527.85
2011.02.02 14:08	0.93436	-9.52	8 544.89
2011.02.02 14:08	0.93433	-9.52	8 562.29
2011.02.02 14:08	1.37844	4.80	3 560.00
2011.02.02 14:08	1.37835	4.80	3 528.00
2011.02.02 14:08	1.37829	4.80	3 440.00
2011.02.02 14:08	1.37814	4.80	3 200.00
2011.02.02 14:08	1.37821	4.80	3 216.00
2011.02.02 14:08	1.37815	4.80	3 056.00
2011.02.02 14:08	1.37816	4.80	3 128.00
2011.02.02 14:09	1.37826	4.80	3 240.00
2011.02.02 14:09	1.37829	4.80	3 392.00
2011.02.02 14:09	1.37831	4.80	3 408.00
2011.02.02 14:09	81.446	-1.48	1 630.53
2011.02.02 14:09	81.446	-1.48	1 718.93
2011.02.02 14:09	81.448	-1.48	1 699.24
2011.02.02 14:09	81.446	-1.48	1 709.11
2011.02.02 14:09	81.451	-1.48	1 659.89
2011.02.02 14:09	81.452	-1.48	1 650.05
2011.02.02 14:09	81.452	-1.48	1 650.05
2011.02.02 14:09	81.450	-1.48	1 669.74
2011.02.02 14:10	81.447	-1.48	1 699.26
2011.02.02 14:10	81.450	-1.48	1 669.74
2011.02.02 14:10	1.61852	0.16	7 240.00
2011.02.02 14:10	1.61856	0.16	7 272.00

3

Don't Get Emotional

Even with the most successful implementation of solid trend identification methodologies, you may still end up among an unfortunate group of people who fail miserably at forex. Of all the people who lose money in forex despite knowledge of proper techniques to win trades, 90% fail because of emotionally motivated decisions.

Forex is highly leveraged. One mistake can be exceptionally costly. The leverage is why winning trades can produce such substantial profits. But, losing trades can also be seriously costly. This is why trusting data and always Trading In The Now is essential.

Measure your own limitations. Maybe it seems that you never make mistakes in life. God bless you. The simple fact is that there are a lot of different market conditions. There are nearly infinite possibilities in terms of time frame and price movement chart combinations. This is why this book teaches principles and guidelines, not absolutes. It's also why this trading system is not and cannot be automated. I can't show you or a computer programmer every possible "set-up" or scenario. I see new things every day in price movement trajectory and time frame velocity combinations.

So, we must acknowledge that there are no fixed rules about trends that we can rely upon to be 100% correct. There are only "probabilities" based on the real time data you see at any given moment within constantly changing global market conditions.

The fundamental distinction between attempting to use Technical or Fundamental Analysis to predict, signal or speculate a future outcome versus calculating a viable statistical probability based on 100% true real time data is, however, the cornerstone innovation of Trajectory Forex.

Technical analysts will show you formations that serve as "signals" for impending profit taking opportunities. There is no such thing as a repeating "signal" that predicts an opportunity to make profits on any consistent basis. Again, if there were such magic and dependable signals, everyone who ever traded forex would be rich.

In fact, most people who have traded forex have lost their money. The primary reason, in my opinion, is that the huge majority of people are given a false sense of confidence in misleading technical indicators. It's predictive. It's the voodoo of constructing future scenarios based on past performance. It doesn't work. Yet, people get into forex utilizing this well developed scam of a methodology, and they quickly find themselves broke or looking at a zero balance in their account. This is why I want to emphasize that the Trajectory Forex methodology is based on statistical "probabilities" – not guarantees – and you must make your own determinations as to when there "might" be a greater or lesser opportunity to take profits.

I will show you examples, but there are no guarantees. Anyone who promises you they can teach you a certain and absolute method to make profits in forex or any other investment market is full of it. Remember, if it sounds too good to be true...

Success in Trajectory Forex hinges on your individual ability to coldly and logically look at price movement in multiple time frame charts, and then make relatively simple, clear cut decisions that I will detail with examples later in this book. You should trust your decisions to make trades that produce profits, but only to the extent that the statistical probabilities you see in real time merit ongoing, and that your Max Loss Rule allows.

This system is not overwhelming or exceptionally difficult to execute. It simply requires an understanding first of the concept of calculating the trajectory and velocity of a moving object (price in this case), and then how to execute trades based on the real time data to win profits. You must always remember that you can and will make trades that are simply wrong. It happens. This is why we seek to always win big, but also only lose small.

The analytical processes within Trajectory Forex will test your personality and your ability to control emotions. In particular, you will have to have a firm grip on your inescapable human sense of greed and the inevitable desire to "get even" after a loss. All of us feel these things. It's just a question as to whether or not you can control your behavior and rise above such emotions to achieve objective, data-driven logical decision making.

How many times have you heard stories of people going broke in places like casinos because they wouldn't leave until they "got even". Your desire to win will NEVER destine you to win. So, if you can control your emotions, accept small losses, and intelligently capture bigger profits when you correctly identify trends, then you will profit on a consistent basis.

Smart money management will produce net profits even if you are trading just based on the flip of a coin. Lose small. Win big. It works even if you're trading at random. Try it in a free demo account. Limit your losses through strict discipline. Ride winning trades for all the profit they will yield. Money management is a skill in and of itself and it consistently produces net profits. It's the reason that I've actually had professional technical traders in forex tell me that they make profits despite averaging, at best, only 40% winning trades. That's right! Even some of the best technical analysts have told me they lose 60% or more of all trades, yet they end the day with net profits. How? Money management.

The real skill successful technical traders have mastered isn't really technical analysis. It's knowing how to be disciplined to such extent that they ONLY lose small, and every win is to the maximum. It's all about the discipline of money management. So, we must assume here that money management is a fundamental you will practice and implement on every trade. It's not difficult to learn. I've already explained the fundamentals. But like most things, money management is all about proper execution on a consistent basis.

Again, success and profitability come down to simple discipline.

Now, when you apply a methodology that actually increases your probability of choosing more winning trades than losing trades, then you should be able to dramatically and rapidly increase profits with implementation of smart money management.

Win big when you win. Lose small when it moves against you. Always.

Lastly, before I get into the pretty basic step-by-step, I want to tell you about disclosure and the IRS. Be honest. Period. Each and every day, set aside 30 -40% of your earnings for the IRS or the appropriate amount for your nation's government taxes. Set up an account with the IRS or appropriate state and national taxing authority, so that you can make regular deposits or simply put the 30 - 40% into a safe investment that pays interest. At the end of the year, you may not actually owe all that you've saved. I'd offer that you should consider that extra end of year cash a performance bonus. But, when dealing with your government taxing authority, it's better to be safe than sorry. (Cause they don't actually accept "sorry" as an excuse, and being on the wrong side of a government taxing authority can definitely be an emotional experience.)

NEVER TRADE FOREX, EARN PROFITS, AND FAIL TO REPORT THEM TO THE GOVERNMENT.

I have to be very serious with you here because it's tempting to think you are under the radar and can't be found. The fact is that, while you're doing your trading on the Internet and it can seem likely no one will notice you and your individual trades in this global $3 trillion per day (and growing) financial marketplace, you have to accept that they will always find out when you are winning profits. No doubt, forex is the planet's biggest financial market. It's worldwide. So, yes, it's easy to think you are invisible.

But, while you and I are fleas on an elephant's back so to speak, the IRS still watches bank accounts for large deposits. When you start depositing money in the range of $1600 to $4000 per day, they will notice. Actually, it is your bank that will notice, and they must report deposit activity at certain levels to the IRS. So just accept that you have to pay your taxes.

I apologize if this sounds like an elementary lecture. I will simply never forget one younger trader who contacted me after learning this system and earning pretty hefty profits for several months. He said, "So, I realized the other day that I'm going to have to pay some serious taxes on this money." I offered that he would indeed have to pay taxes and I asked why he hadn't already started planning for them. He replied, "Honestly, I was expecting to lose it all back. I've never won consistently in forex."

Once you learn Trajectory Forex and you start earning profits, start planning for taxes. Don't wait till you're six months into the process. Don't wait for some magical curse to hit you because you've always failed in forex before. Definitely don't wait till the end of a year has passed. Save and plan from the start.

From the first day you start producing profits, put your 30 - 40% on deposit or (better yet) work with a CPA to manage your obligations and be very smartly organized for taxes. Most importantly, do what you have to do in order to enjoy peace of mind and keep trading. Hopefully, most of the money you put aside will end up coming back to you at the end of the year.

ALWAYS CONSULT A CERTIFIED PUBLIC ACCOUNTANT OR ATTORNEY TO DETERMINE EXACTLY HOW MUCH YOU SHOULD PAY IN TAXES.

THE AUTHOR IS NOT A TAX AUTHORITY, TAX ADVISOR OR EXPERT. THE AUTHOR REFERENCES 30 TO 40% TAX WITHHOLDINGS BECAUSE THIS IS THE AUTHOR'S SUBJECTIVE ESTIMATE OF WHAT A PROFITABLE TRADER MIGHT PAY IN TAXES BASED UPON THE AUTHOR'S EXPERIENCE BUT WITH NO KNOWLEDGE OF TAX LAW. AFTER DEDUCTIONS AND OTHER EXPENSES, AN INDIVIDUAL TRADER MAY BE OBLIGATED TO PAY MORE OR LESS IN TAXES.

YOUR TAX SITUATION DEPENDS ON YOUR INDIVIDUAL CIRCUMSTANCES. ALWAYS CONSULT AN EXPERT TO ASSURE YOU WITHHOLD THE CORRECT AMOUNT OF MONEY FOR THE IRS AND/OR YOUR LOCAL GOVERNMENT TAXING AUTHORITIES. THE AUTHOR ASSUMES NO RESPONSIBILITY FOR YOUR TAX OBLIGATIONS AND MAKES NO REPRESENTATION THAT ANY MENTION OF TAXES OR SUGGESTIONS RELATIVE TO TAX OBLIGATIONS MIGHT, IN FACT, APPLY TO YOU. YOU AND YOU ALONE ARE RESPONSIBLE FOR ALL LOCAL, STATE AND FEDERAL TAXES.

SOLID PROFITS ON A SMALL ACCOUNT

Price	Swap	Profit
0.84000	-1.05	732.65
1.21997	-2.45	93.00
1.21997	-2.45	74.00
1.22632	-0.70	940.00
0.84692	-0.70	701.00
0.83220	-0.71	1 082.81
1.22408	-0.70	810.00
0.83721	0.00	293.77
1.22999	0.00	314.00
0.83500	-2.12	102.23
0.83504	-2.12	78.87
1.22550	0.00	382.00
1.22150	0.00	408.00
0.83660	0.62	269.72
1.22271	0.00	46.00
0.83586	0.00	81.93
1.22283	0.00	18.00
1.22303	0.00	48.00
1.22150	0.00	158.00
1.22146	0.00	128.00
0.83384	0.00	134.60

Trajectory Forex

1.22049	0.00	166.00
0.83383	0.00	114.10
1.21959	0.00	120.00
1.22021	0.00	92.00
0.83282	0.00	251.67
1.21919	0.00	36.00
1.21767	0.00	272.00
1.21871	0.00	188.00
1.21681	-0.70	136.00
0.83215	-0.70	157.89
1.21683	-0.70	522.00
1.20550	0.00	6 732.00
0.82687	0.00	2 980.99
		19 254.14

4.

Brokers and Software

Next, as we get into Trajectory Forex, you should download the software platform that works best for trading currencies and learn how to use it. Fortunately, the software is easy to find. Just visit any search engine on your computer and enter the following search term: forex trading software downloads. The current software is MT4. MT5 is coming out soon if not already available, or so I've been told.

What you will get is a long list of brokers offering free downloadable MT4 or MT5 software that you can use on your PC to trade foreign currency. I also believe this software works on the current generation of Macs. When I started, I had to buy a PC in order to use the software. As a Mac guy, I am glad to see this change. But, I still use the basic software on a PC...force of successful habit.

Bottom line, a PC may likely still give you more options to use software from different brokers, but you can today find software that will work on the latest generations of Mac.

Beware the loads of scam offers, overnight "get rich quick" schemes and EA trading robots you will see pop up the minute you type the word forex into your search engine.

Forex is the single most profitable financial market on the planet. It has been widely documented that most banks, corporations and major investors make more money trading forex than any other investment activity. Because so much money can be made so fast, it has attracted scam artists of every description. They will try to sell you everything from trading signal services to Expert Advisor (EA) automated trading robots, and they will promise you great riches almost instantly. In my experience, none of these systems or trading robots work consistently. I promise you that just about everything you see on Forex promising overnight riches is likely a scam. Save your money.

Here is all you need to know to enjoy a little confidence in Trajectory Forex. It is based on the mathematics of observing and calculating the movement of an object in space. Trajectory Forex is about the physics that apply to every moving object in our universe. It's also openly acknowledged to be based on statistical probabilities versus absolutes. There are no guarantees of success. That is, at the least, honest.

Trajectory Forex is grounded in a solid foundation of data analysis. We focus only on pure price movement and the time it takes for said price movements, which identifies speed of motion with 100% true, real time data. In this way, we are determining the trajectory and velocity of a virtual object in constant motion: a currency price. We are then making informed calculations and qualitative trading decisions on the probability of continued momentum. Every decision is based on information that is known to be indisputably true at all times.

Trajectory Forex is different from any other trend identification method widely implemented today. It is unique in the respect that it does not rely on any other indicators, interpretive or predictive variables such as you find in Technical Analysis. All the data you need for Trajectory Forex streams into your MT4 trading platform live in real time.

Price movement in forex, the stock market or any other trading environment can be looked at in the same way that you observe any object in motion in the universe. The mathematics of trajectory calculation are also the only reliable way to consistently identify the direction and velocity of movement for any given object (real or virtual). Historical data used to predict movement, interpretations of outside influences, and other speculations are going to fail more often than succeed. Even predicting the movement of the Earth is a matter of statistical probability, because we do not know if an asteroid is going to hit within the next six hours and change everything.

Will the sun rise tomorrow morning? It's a statistical probability…not a guarantee!

The mathematics of trajectory calculation are the only viable path to honestly, consistently, and with a high degree of repeated accuracy identifying the high statistical probability of ongoing movement of a price (or any object) in any system. This is why Trajectory Forex is the primary way to identify trends for profit.

As you learn the system by reading this book, you might as well select a specific broker now and prepare to use their MT4 platform in order to make trades in demo mode. As you study details on subsequent pages, it will help you to be able to turn to your PC and see a chart with price movement happening right before your eyes. There are also screen shots of time frames and price movement on subsequent pages, so it's helpful to be able to see the real thing on your computer as you read along. It's just a suggestion. You can also read the book twice, or go back and forth. That's your choice.

Two places you might find worthwhile in looking for the right broker as I write this book are: www.MT4Spreads.com and www.100forexbrokers.com/compare-forex-brokers-spreads. I am not affiliated in any way with either of these websites, but they currently report brokers and their spreads (which is the cost you pay for every trade). I do not endorse any of the brokers on these websites, and I don't honestly want to endorse ANY broker. So please consider any reference to a broker in this book as mere observation. It is not advice. I am not affiliated with any broker, nor do I accept responsibility for the behavior of a broker. You must also choose a broker with whom you can trade legally in your nation of residence. For me, after the bank collapses in the United States in 2007, I definitely observe that one can just about trust no business or financial institution beyond a certain point.

So, all I can do is point you in some directions that "look" right to me at time of writing this book. The final decision as to where you trade your money is your decision and your decision alone. This is also true of those two websites: www.MT4Spreads.com and www.100forexbrokers.com/compare-forex-brokers-spreads. If either or both disappear tomorrow or provide inaccurate information, just check the Internet for other references. There are nearly countless resources where you can find information on different brokers. Indeed, there's so much information that it almost becomes confusing. Sometimes, especially at the start, it's simply smart to pick the first broker who seems reasonable, practice in demo with them, and make a final broker selection when it's time for you to trade with cash.

It should take you about a month of practice before you feel ready to trade and win profits with cash. Of course, this is just an estimate based on people who have learned this system from me in the past few years. Everyone's different. You may read this book and be ready to go in a couple days. It might also take you a couple months before you feel enough confidence to risk cash. It's entirely based on your individual learning curve. The positive point here is that the methodology is one that you can learn and use to earn profits. So stick with it!

Please just remember that I am not responsible for your broker or any other choices you make as to how you trade your money. I'm trying to give you a set of tools with which you can build a house of financial wealth. If the roof caves in because you didn't study the structural design section, I can't be responsible for your construction techniques (or your actual trading practices). Does that make sense? If not, there's a huge, long, legal disclaimer at the end of this book. So please read it.

You must know that forex is risky (any investing is risky), and you trade at your own risk. You should also never trade money you can't afford to lose. Why? The main reason is that you'll make bad decisions because of the inherent emotions. So, if you can set aside some money that you can afford to lose, fine. If you're trading this month's mortgage payment, however, bad idea. You'll likely fail just based on the influence of the emotions at play.

Among the many worthy brokers you'll find out there as I write this book are GoMarkets (www.gomarketsaus.com) and iamFX (www.iamfx.com), but not all brokers I mention can do business with U.S. citizens due to regulatory matters. A lot of other great brokers also offer superior spreads compared to competitors and provide great service. You may also want to look at some of today's biggest brokers, and among them are FX Pro in the UK (www.fxpro.com) and Alpari (www.alpari-us.com for U.S. traders, and www.alpari.co.uk for rest of world).

There are countless brokers based in the United States, but I do not recommend one domestic U.S. broker over another. There are a lot of regulatory matters currently transpiring in the U.S., so it's best for me to simply let you make your own decisions. Suffice to say, as of this writing, you can use the Trajectory Forex manual trend identification methodology with any forex broker in the United States as well as any broker around the world.

I must offer that you have to be careful in selecting a broker to assure you get someone who's legitimate and honest. It's also typically best to choose someone with a long and established history, as well as some size. Bigger brokers are likely more stable and safe than smaller brokers.

After the collapse of some big banks in the U.S. a few years ago, there are not many institutions I totally trust. Thus, you should never leave your entire account balance on deposit with any single broker. As you build your wealth, distribute that money in multiple accounts with different brokers. Also pull a large portion of profits out of the system regularly for safe keeping. That's just smart and conservative, especially in these unstable economic times.

Here are a few key questions to ask any forex broker before opening a cash account when the time comes.

1. Do they hold your funds to trade against their own reserves, or do they pass your funds straight through to the world population of banks? (You want the broker who commits in writing to pass your funds through to the banks versus possibly holding your trades in-house which creates a conflict of interest.)

2. Do they offer 100 to 1 leverage, or are they limited to 50 to 1 leverage as regulated by the CFTC in the U.S.? (100 to 1 is better,

but you can still earn substantial profits with 50 to 1. If possible, find a broker who's not regulated by the CFTC if you're trading in the United States. Again, I'm not sure if there are any U.S. brokers remaining today who are not regulated by the CFTC. The regulations are constantly being changed. If you end up trading 50 to 1 leverage in the U.S., however, don't worry. You can still build your account with consistent winning trades.)

3. How many years have they been in business, and do they have any members of their executive team or board of directors who are directly affiliated or active participants with the NFA, CFTC or any other government regulatory agency? (You must avoid all conflicts of interest, so avoid anyone who admits they have someone on their board or a member of their executive team who's also affiliated in a formal capacity with a government regulatory agency. This is just a personal preference of mine, but I think it's wise to avoid conflicts of interest.)

I don't trust all brokers, and that includes a number who look to be large and secure. You have to make your own decisions on this one. Endorsing a broker here would be like endorsing a bank before 2007 happened in the U.S. All I can really suggest is that you trust no one beyond a reasonable point, and do your own homework to research credibility before making cash deposits.

One resource I have personally come to trust is Forex Peace Army (www.forexpeacearmy.com). The observations and advice there are free, and they offer a lot of helpful information online. Perhaps the best reason I can suggest to substantiate their credibility to a fair extent is the fact that a large community of forex traders communicate openly on forums at Forex Peace Army. Keep in mind this also means everyone with an opinion speaks out. The best use for Forex Peace Army, in my opinion, is in the reviews of brokers versus believing every opinion expressed in a forum. Believe me, everyone has an opinion.

As for doing business with brokers, always read every word of information the broker must legally provide to you on their websites and in the disclosures you will get before opening a live (cash) account. It will give you a good idea about how your money is going to be handled. What you are looking for is a broker who will commit to you that they will pass your funds through to the world population of banks, create no delays in execution of trades other than real market behaviors, and never hold your funds in-house trading them against their own cash reserves. If you can do business with a dealer versus a broker, it's usually a smart choice. But that's also just my personal opinion. You can find out the difference between a forex dealer and a forex broker with a simple search on the web.

Now, let's get back to your education on forex.

Spreads are the cost you pay to the broker for every trade you make in forex. The spread is a fraction of a pip (a fraction of a penny), so it's not a large cost. I repeatedly tell my traders not to worry about the cost of spreads. As we learn more and more about identifying trends via calculation of trajectory, we will quickly be able to earn profits that far outpace the cost of spreads. So, don't be a tightwad. Accept that paying the broker his spread is just the cost of doing business in forex. It's no big deal. Your profits will make it worthwhile, and you'll be glad to reward your broker with his spreads in exchange for access to this global trading marketplace.

Also keep in mind, relative to the specific brokers that I've mentioned; I'm offering these suggestions at the time of writing this book with full knowledge that things change on the Internet and in the forex market every single day. If any of the above links are outdated or if brokers merge or disappear because they get bought out by some other broker, please don't despair and don't blame me. I'm writing about a trading methodology. I don't have future insight into changes in the market, government regulations, or status of individual brokers and dealers.

If things change, just get on a good search engine and look for a new broker. Most allow international customers. Some nations prefer for you to trade domestically, like the United States. But you'll be okay with a U.S. broker if you learn Trajectory trend identification properly.

Education is paramount, because the singular goal is to consistently win trades.

Statistically, about 80% of all consumer traders in forex actually lose all their money. So don't trade forex until and unless you know what you're doing. Read this book. Practice on a demo account (where no money is at risk). Learn how to identify trends that produce a net profit, and at least double one demo account before even thinking about opening a live cash account with a broker.

The Trajectory Forex trend identification methodology will work on any trading platform and it will work not only in forex but any other market where prices change on a regular basis. So, for instance, you could use the Trajectory methodology to trade on the New York Stock Exchange. Since the system fundamentally identifies trends via calculation of trajectory and price movement velocity, there are no special requirements in order to implement this system. Whatever information platform you choose or whatever market you trade, this methodology should work if price movement data is available in real time.

Now, let's discuss the importance of your state of mind when trading.

You cannot succeed if you are stressed or emotionally challenged during the process of trend identification. You must be logical, relaxed, cool and calm in order to succeed in trading forex, and this especially includes implementation of the Trajectory Forex methodology. So learn some ways to control your emotions and stay calm. A relaxed trader is a successful trader. The most successful traders actually find a way to stop thinking about every pip they win as money. They start to see it almost as if it's a game, and they are scoring points versus losing points. When you are constantly adding up how much money you've just won or lost, you distract yourself from the process of analyzing the real time data that reveals trend movement.

There will be time enough for counting when the trading's done. Or something like that, right?

ONCE YOU HAVE YOUR MT4 TRADING PLATFORM SOFTWARE, OPEN A DEMO ACCOUNT AND PRACTICE BEFORE YOU TRADE WITH CASH!

This is mandatory. The number one goal in forex or any other investment market is to simply avoid losing money. If you are an active investor and you avoid losing money, you have achieved the first and most important goal in the endeavor to make profits.

With forex, you have two things to learn. First, you must learn how to utilize the MT4 trading platform. It is relatively simple, but you need to be comfortable using this basic software. Second, you must learn the Trajectory Forex trend identification methodology.

So, open a practice account and make the system work first with play money in demo mode. When you prove to yourself that you can do this consistently and you've at least doubled one demo account, then you are ready to make some serious profits.

In terms of learning the MT4 platform, I will not get into specific details here. There are very little if any differences from one broker's software to another, so the best way to learn the software is by talking to your broker if you have questions. Most large brokers have FAQ sections on their website, and they are very glad to teach you how to learn their MT4 trading platform. Most brokers also have online chat options, so you can ask questions and get quick answers. It's not difficult, and thus doesn't really require a lot of explanation here. But learn how to work the platform. Make trades in demo.

If you want to learn how to drive a car, get behind the wheel. The same truth applies here. If you want to trade forex, download a platform and start making trades in demo mode.

START WINNING TRADES CONSISTENTLY

Price	Swap	Profit
0.84692	-0.70	701.00
0.84000	-1.05	732.65
0.83500	-1.05	1 468.74
1.22999	0.00	314.00
0.83721	0.00	293.77
0.83220	-0.71	1 082.81
1.22408	-0.70	810.00
1.22150	0.00	408.00

1.22550	0.00	382.00
0.83660	0.62	269.72
1.22271	0.00	46.00
1.22283	0.00	18.00
1.22303	0.00	48.00
0.83586	0.00	81.93
1.21997	-2.45	93.00
1.21997	-2.45	74.00
0.83500	-2.12	102.23
0.83504	-2.12	78.87
1.22150	0.00	158.00
1.22146	0.00	128.00
1.22049	0.00	166.00
1.22021	0.00	92.00
0.83384	0.00	134.60
0.83383	0.00	114.10
1.21959	0.00	120.00
1.21919	0.00	36.00
1.21767	0.00	272.00
		8 524.69

5

Real Time Data

No matter how good a system is in step-by-step design, you must still execute every step correctly. Practice is essential.

Trend identification via the Trajectory method requires an element of analysis as you look at the data. While, in many cases, trends will be somewhat easy to identify with the variables we explain in this book, you can make mistakes…especially if you are trading with the short term in mind or just impatient and trying to make some quick, small profits with the misguided assumption that you can move only on short term data (like M1 and M5 time frames alone). That's a scalping philosophy, but it disregards the longer term time frames that show every aspect of the true trajectory and its ongoing velocity.

Still, this is a critical mistake routinely made by greedy newcomers who falsely believe that all you need is short term movement. Trading on the last couple minutes of price movement without consideration for longer term trajectory and velocity is a recipe for disaster.

I will not say it's impossible for a trader to move fast on small or low probability micro trends. But you must be aware of what you are doing at all times relative to all time frames, and longer term trends (or absence of trends long term).

Equally important, always limit your losses by watching shorter term movement. Know that this system will give you indicators of potential profit opportunities at varying degrees of strength. This means the success rate in terms of statistical probability will vary depending on how aggressive you are in going after profit taking opportunities.

Don't get too aggressive at first. Don't take too many high risks until you have traded long enough to truly understand the difference between high and low risk scenarios. Try to stay conservative at least in the first few months of cash trading when you start.

You should not be responsible for losses that may exceed the amount of money you have in your account, but always communicate with your broker on their individual rules. The rules are always subject to change one broker to the next.

Some brokers are implementing new rules to cover "potential" losses. So make sure to pick up the phone and talk to your broker. Communicate with your broker. Ask them to CONFIRM that all you have at risk is the actual amount of money in your account! Even if this is an international call, TALK to your broker before opening the cash account. Use Skype or just pay for the phone call. But talk to your broker.

Beware the brokers who attempt to make you responsible for "potential" losses beyond what you have in your account. Think about it. Why would a broker need to implement such a policy? If they simply pass your money through to the world population of banks and merely take their spread up front, which is the agreed upon compensation for a broker, how in the world might you be at risk for more than you have on deposit?

One reason, as just my own personal speculation with no intent to indict any broker specifically, is my belief that a broker might possibly be holding your money and trading it against their own reserves. In most cases, new traders are using flawed trend identification methodologies like Technical Analysis or EA robots that don't work long term, so they lose most of their trades. This means the broker can trade your money against their own cash reserves. Never put your money into the actual forex market, and then just pocket every dime you traded when you lose! But what if you pick a winner that exceeds what they can pay you? What if the move in your favor happens in mere seconds before they can put that position in place in the outside market?

That's just my own skeptical speculation about what a broker "might" do. The fact that I'm also aware that some brokers absolutely do engage in this unethical practice is another matter, and I'm not going to name names. Let's just say that you should ask the question and make sure your money is truly sent through by the broker into the world's population of forex trading banks.

This is a simple business. If the broker starts making it sound overly complicated or if they impose unusual liabilities on you beyond the amount you have on deposit in your account, don't trade with that broker. Period.

This means that a phone conversation with your broker is not optional. It's mandatory. Be smart. Be clear on the broker's rules. No matter how good the Trajectory Forex trend identification methodology is in actual performance, you must know the rules in place with your broker. Would you play a game or sport without full knowledge of all the rules? No. Would you play a professional sport where you suspected the officials were imposing rules with a bias against you, or had a conflict of interest? No.

So don't trade your money with a broker unless you know all the rules with 100% clarity, and this includes every minor detail and variation that might be applied. Make a phone call to discuss questions with your broker before you trade any cash. Make sure to investigate the possibility of opening a live account with several large brokers simply to become familiar with rules and regulations. Then select the correct broker with whom to invest.

PUT MULTIPLE TRADES ON A WINNING TREND

Time	Price	Swap	Profit
2011.01.21 18:32	0.95782	-1.32	6 548.20
2011.01.21 18:32	0.95782	-1.32	6 372.80
2011.01.21 18:32	1.59999	0.16	10 240.00
2011.01.21 18:32	1.59994	0.16	10 176.00
2011.01.21 18:32	1.59979	0.16	10 040.00
2011.01.21 18:32	1.59979	0.16	10 032.00
2011.01.21 18:32	1.59984	0.16	10 120.00
2011.01.21 18:32	1.35972	1.20	12 416.00
2011.01.21 18:32	1.35972	1.20	12 424.00
2011.01.21 18:32	1.35970	1.20	12 344.00
2011.01.21 18:32	1.35972	1.20	12 304.00
2011.01.21 18:30	1.35961	1.20	12 216.00
2011.01.21 18:30	1.35961	1.20	12 216.00
2011.01.21 18:30	1.35961	1.20	12 248.00
2011.01.21 18:30	1.35960	1.20	12 208.00
2011.01.21 18:30	1.35951	1.20	12 128.00
2011.01.21 18:30	1.35950	1.20	12 080.00
2011.01.24 18:56	1.36391	1.20	3 328.00
2011.01.24 18:56	1.36394	1.20	3 376.00
2011.01.24 18:56	1.36395	1.20	3 384.00
2011.01.24 18:56	1.36395	1.20	3 384.00
2011.01.24 18:57	1.36411	1.20	3 472.00
2011.01.24 18:57	1.36416	1.20	3 536.00
2011.01.24 18:57	1.36410	1.20	3 488.00
2011.01.24 18:57	1.36414	1.20	3 568.00
2011.01.24 18:57	1.36420	1.20	3 624.00
2011.01.24 18:57	1.36420	1.20	3 624.00
2011.01.24 18:57	0.94845	-1.33	7 844.38
2011.01.24 18:57	0.94845	-1.33	7 844.38
2011.01.24 18:57	0.94845	-1.33	7 844.38
2011.01.24 18:57	0.94846	-1.33	7 827.43
2011.01.24 18:57	0.94846	-1.33	7 818.99
2011.01.24 18:57	0.94847	-1.33	7 810.47
2011.01.24 18:57	0.94848	-1.33	7 801.96

2011.01.24 18:57	0.94844	0.00	5 516.43
2011.01.25 20:07	0.94269	-1.34	10 378.81
2011.01.25 20:07	0.94272	-1.34	10 471.83
2011.01.25 20:07	0.94271	-1.34	10 454.96
2011.01.25 20:07	0.94270	-1.34	10 573.88
2011.01.25 20:07	0.94269	-1.34	10 590.97
2011.01.25 20:08	0.94271	-1.34	10 497.40

6

Price Trajectory And Probability

The Trajectory Forex system was originally developed as a momentum scalping technique when I first started trading forex in 2006.

I observed in real time data that currencies which move 100 pips would, with high statistical probability, continue to hit 103 – 105 pips. This had nothing to do with the time it took for the currency to move 100 pips (or velocity of price movement). It was simply the sheer power and momentum indicated by this one piece of data: total pips of price movement.

This remains true today, although the risks of trading that original system are significantly higher in the current unstable global economy. Statistically and historically, about 97% of all trades that move 100 pips will continue an additional 3 – 5 pips, and this allows you to make a profit on top of the cost of the spread. Unfortunately, it can take a couple days before you see a movement of 100 pips or more. Or you might today see a swing of 100 pips up and down in five minutes.

If you were hedging, as I did in my original system but is not necessary in today's Trajectory methodology, you would have opened a buy and a sell on a currency pair, and simply waited for the stop on the losing side to be hit at 100 pips, and then the limit (or take profit) would be hit at 103 – 105 pips worth of movement depending on the spread and difference in price when I opened both the buy and the sell. These trades won profits exclusively due to the momentum of price movement disregarding time (speed of movement). This methodology remains a somewhat viable, documented statistical phenomenon when you can legally hedge.

Note that, as of today, you can hedge in every nation on the planet except the United States thanks to a National Futures Association (NFA) regulation that was put in place during 2009 to "protect" the American consumer. No further comment.

In any event, in several years of back testing on this original system, we also found that trades at a 360 pip range for the stops (363 to 365 for take profit limits) achieved 100% success with just minor variation in the range depending on the currency. In other words, you would never see a currency go up or down 300 pips, then (at that exact point) reverse by 600 pips and hit both the buy and sell stops on a hedge. We simply never saw it happen in back testing on any currency at 360+ pips.

So the original system I used was simple and effective. It produced one to two pips profit per trade and evidenced the power of price movement alone as an indicator of momentum.

As the market started to change in late 2007, with banks in the U.S. collapsing and other global economies becoming increasingly unstable, I began to notice a lot more sideways movement. The market became consolidated. Consolidation in financial markets initially means there is little trend movement. That's the first thing I noticed, and it challenged my initial system for making money in forex. But, the second thing that typically happens in a highly consolidated financial market is that it actually becomes very unstable. Instead of mere sideways movement (non-trend movement), you start to see a lot of swings up and down.

This has been the typical condition of the Forex market for the past couple years. Still, by applying time as a second variable in concert with price movement, I was able to see the trajectory of price movement as well as its velocity. This allowed me to better identify the real time momentum of price movement at any given point. Suddenly, with the identification of price movement trajectory and velocity, I could identify profit taking opportunities even in the unstable global marketplace!

It was a profound revelation, because the birth of Trajectory trend identification transcended every other methodology I had ever heard about in forex. This was something new. Simple in concept, but legitimate and remarkably successful in identifying profit opportunities both long range and short term.

When you add the second variable, time frame, which identifies the SPEED of price movement, then you seriously elevate the quality of data-based analysis and open the opportunity for significantly bigger profits via consistent identification of trend momentum in real time.

Utilizing two real time 100% true pieces of data suddenly becomes the key to substantial, long term profitability. You must learn the art and science of synthesizing price movement data in real time aggregate pips with the streaming flow of time frames that show total pips worth of movement per minute, per hour, per day, per week and per month. But this is the simplicity of the system. Essentially, this is the innovation of Trajectory Forex.

With this information, I was now able to observe price movement in multiple time frame charts and evaluate whether or not a currency was going to have continued movement in the same direction with a high statistical probability.

The discovery of Trajectory Forex changed everything in my world of finance. I hope it opens a world of opportunity for you as I detail more in the coming pages.

While no other Technical or Fundamental Analysis techniques proved consistently successful in identifying profit taking opportunities for me, Trajectory Forex demonstrated a profound tendency to consistently identify the momentum of price movement, and thus a very high success rate.

7

Two True Variables

I have often referred to Trajectory Forex trend identification as "two variable" or "no stop/no limit" trading. This is because you are utilizing two and only two 100% true pieces of real time data and the point at which the profit taking ends is determined by the market...not pre-determined by you setting a stop or limit. You "may" set a trailing stop, but I typically don't bother. If I have a trade that's live, I am going to sit there and watch it until the profit taking ends. No need for stops and limits. When we trade, we stay in front of our computers while the trade is live and exposed.

The two most important pieces of information in forex are price movement and time frames of movement. These are the two pieces of data we know to be 100% true at all times. They are the keys to identifying trend movement of price or the trajectory of a currency, and thus revealing the momentum or causal effects fueling the movement that yields profits.

This same data is used in physics to calculate the trajectory of any moving object in three dimensional space. If a football player kicks a football into the air (pure evaluation of an initial causal effect and then the statistical probability of continued momentum in flight), or if NASA launches a satellite into space (the rocket being the causal effect that fuels upward movement), measurement of speed and direction of motion will allow you to calculate and plot the object's exact trajectory at any point in time.

First, you look at velocity in terms of vertical and horizontal movement. This is one dimensional measurement of directional movement. Second, you choose a value for time, and calculate the horizontal and vertical distances traveled in a given period of time (such as feet per second, or miles per hour, or pips per minute/hour/day). This is the basic concept behind how you calculate the velocity or speed, and determine the trajectory.

There actually is an exceptionally complex mathematical formula for calculating true trajectory, but I'm not going to get into it here because it confuses more than it resolves for nearly everyone except college professors and mathematicians. Feel free to look it up and apply to forex price movement trajectory if you wish. I'm always in favor of more mathematics versus less. But most people aren't going to be able to handle that formula. You will find, however, that the formula and explanations behind it incorporate time and speed of motion, which is exactly what we're evaluating in price movement and time frame charts.

A faster moving object (one that is covering more feet per second in a specific direction relative to horizontal/vertical) will go higher and farther than a slower moving object. The feet per second or miles per second measured over an extended period of time, or pips per minute, pips per hour, pips per day reveal the velocity with a deeper perspective (which is exceptionally valuable and transcends typical trajectory calculations which are often based on a snapshot of an object's movement at a particular moment versus observations over multiple, extended time frames).

What this means is that we can observe and calculate a clear and accurate picture of price movement trajectory through observation of movement over different time periods. In the process, you will identify the presence or absence of strong and relatively constant velocity of movement, which reveals causal effects driving the observed price movement. Collectively, these two quantitative variables allow you to make a qualitative determination of the statistical probability that this trend of movement will or will not continue in the same direction.

Is this data 100% true in identifying every price movement trend in every instance? Yes. The data is actually 100% accurate on a ongoing basis. The challenge is evaluating this real time data relative to statistical probabilities of continued movement on the same trajectory. There are also the inevitable changes in causal effects that can alter a trajectory regardless of the observed movement up to any point in time.

As I noted earlier, there are no 100% guarantees at any given moment. We live in a universe filled with infinite possibilities. This means, no matter how high the probability of continued movement in one direction, things can change. For example, we can observe a dog running at top speed for 20 yards and we can calculate that every single foot he travels happened in mere seconds. What we cannot see, as we evaluate his direction and speed, is the hostile cat that will jump into his path in the 24th yard. The dog may, because of this external causal effect, suddenly change direction and/or velocity. Always remember, we cannot see into the future. We cannot anticipate what "could" happen in the next day or in the next five minutes or in the next five seconds.

Causal effects of literally any nature from anywhere in the world can change the trajectory of price movement in an instant. This is why we implement the max loss rule, and this is why we do not leave an exposed trade alone for even one second. When you make the buy or sell, you stay in front of the computer until you end your profit taking or until the run comes to an end and you get out.

There are no exceptions.

If the football is kicked into the air, and we calculate feet per second of motion through several different consecutive time periods of fractions of a second, then we can calculate a statistically probable forward trajectory at any given moment. But, what if a gust of wind impacts the ball from the rear moments AFTER we take our measurements? The ball may take off on a new trajectory if the wind hits it from behind with strong force. The ball may also change trajectory in another direction if the wind hits it strongly from the front or side. What if there is a sudden downpour of rain? Velocity and trajectory are routinely impacted by changes in real world conditions.

If we launch our rocket into space, there may be changes in the atmosphere that impact the trajectory as calculated at any point in time during the initial phase of flight even with a powerful rocket as the causal effect (real world events propelling our price movement). What will happen when the object launched into space passes through an unexpected jet stream of fast moving air currents, or starts to be released from the Earth's gravity? Trajectory will change even with the powerful rocket (causal effect) supposedly fueling continued movement.

Fortunately, we will see the change in trajectory as it starts to happen. So this is all about observable real world events or "causal effects" that impact trajectory both at the start of a trend and at any point during the trend.

The same is true in using two variables of streaming, real time data in Trajectory Forex to calculate the trajectory of price movement. We know the up and down movement in terms of pips. We also know the time period it took to travel X pips for the past several minutes, hours, days, weeks and months. We can even look at a real time stream of data tick by tick and see the direction of movement as it is happening to the most minute degree possible. Is the price movement continuing in the same direction at relatively the same speed as it has for the past several minutes? Several hours? Several days? Weeks? Months? How important is relatively constant velocity and consistent trajectory to our trust that a causal effect (no matter what it may be) will continue to propel or conversely alter this trajectory?

In reality, we never know what causal effects may happen in the next split second to impact the trajectory of price movement with any currency. How could anyone have anticipated the change in trajectory for currency prices relative to the USD (U.S. Dollar) minutes after two planes crashed into the Twin Towers in New York City on 9/11? This was a tragic event. We would never underestimate the human price of this event. But, for the sake of our purpose here, we can look at this causal effect and see that it dramatically altered the trajectory of price movement in a split second. No one could have foreseen the event. This is just one example of how real world causal effects can change every right, proper and correct calculation you make in terms of trajectory trend identification.

Please note, of course, this is not to say that it takes something massive like terrorist planes hitting twin towers to change trajectory of price movement. An announcement of government financial data in the U.S., or a riot in the streets of Paris, or an oil spill in the waters off the coast of China, or instability in the Middle East are only a few of the endless possible world events that could serve as high impact causal effects on price movement velocity and trajectory.

Equally significant, no single world event impacts price movement by itself. All world events have collective effects, and they balance each other out, negate each other, combine effects, and fundamentally have a collective impact that far transcends any normal consumer's ability to realistically interpret world events in the collective to determine price movement trajectory.

No historical chart patterns, as already discussed relative to technical analysis, can be depended upon to "predict" what price movement trajectory will be seen in the next five minutes or the next five days or the next five months. I hope this explanation has forever dispelled any notion that Technical Analysis can "predict" price movement. So, please, forever forget everything you know about Technical Analysis. It is total voodoo, and will lead the average trader to lose every penny invested (absent extraordinary money management skills, which I would still suggest are more wisely applied to this empirical, data-based Trajectory system versus Technical Analysis).

So. What do we have in order to make profits in forex?

We have two pieces of real time data that give us the constant ability to look at price movement from multiple points of view via different time frames. Our data is continuously updated second by second. It is happening too fast for mathematical calculation by conventional means in my opinion, and I've yet to see software that can effectively calculate price movement trajectory on a consistent, long term basis. So, in brief, we do not have an EA (Expert Advisor) despite the seeming logic of it. You'd think this could be automated, but I have had several people work on this one and no one's been able to get it to work in an EA. One noteworthy fellow who is a veteran software developer for things I cannot detail in this book recently told me he thought he could do it. He is still working on the job, but has not come up with a solution.

One thought today is that it can't be done within a primitive EA, and may require a separate piece of software that possibly runs in the background on your computer and feeds information to a conventional EA without being seen by the broker. That's pretty complex stuff, but we're working on it. Suffice to say, the trajectory formula calculations required are beyond any conventional Expert Advisor software framework in existence.

Thus, Trajectory Forex is a process of human interpretation of the statistical probability that a price movement will or will not continue based on what is observed in real time at any given moment. Trading decisions are made based on the price movement trajectory and velocity that is seen in the multiple time frame charts. Each time frame has different meaning.

Foundation Time Frames

H1, M30 and M15 are the time frames we use in order to see what we believe is the most reliable data on the CURRENT price movement trajectory. Most of the time, you can make initial decisions whether or not to even bother looking at other time frames on a currency pair based on what you see here. These are the Foundation Time Frames we use for initial identification of a trend. If it's not here with velocity, then it's likely not to be seen on this day. So you move on to another currency pair.

Strength Indicator Time Frames

H4, Daily, Weekly, and Monthly are the time frames we use to confirm or question what is observed in H1, M30 and M15. In these longer term time frames, we hope to see alignment of same direction trend price movement to a high and steady velocity (or substantially higher number of total pips worth of movement in one direction versus total pips of movement in retraces the other direction). If we find trajectory alignment to a higher number of total pips, without prolonged sideways movement or questionable velocity, then you have more strength behind the trend you identified in the Foundation Time Frames. That's a good thing. Absence of alignment (disagreement or movement in the opposite direction, sideways, or simply too few pips of same direction movement) means there is less strength behind the trend you observed.

Absence of trajectory alignment and/or velocity in the Strength Indicator Time Frames does not mean you will absolutely fail to find a trading opportunity on this day. A lot of money can be made on profit opportunities that exist only in H1, M30 and M15. But, if you see the same strong trend of price movement trajectory in H4, Daily, Weekly and Monthly time frames, then you have something special. This is likely a price movement trajectory that has some forceful causal effects perpetuating velocity, creating momentum, and likely to continue driving the price in the same direction. It's not absolute because nothing is 100% guaranteed, but it's the closest you will get to a sure thing. Perfect alignment with sustained speed is rare, however, so don't expect to find this often.

This is where the human analytical factor comes into play. You will likely find elements of support in one or another Strength Indicator Time Frame. This is where you must make some qualitative decisions in terms of the viability of the trend. Directional alignment and strong velocity in all longer term Strength Indicator Time Frames is NOT necessary. You are most commonly looking just for some measure of support, or (from another perspective) no major disagreements. The latter may be the most important observation of all.

Short Term Trading Time Frames

M1 and M5 time frames are used primarily to make decisions relative to when you want to get in or out of a trade. They serve as first indicators of sideways movement or retraces that can reveal slowing of price movement trajectory or sudden intervention of a new causal effect. Routinely and consistently, these Short Term Trading Time

Frames are the first places you will see that there "may" be an end to the observed trend movement starting to take place. This could be a minor retrace, or it could be a major reversal.

The number of pips you can afford to lose based on your Max Loss Rule will determine whether or not you have to make fast decisions based on these Short Term Trading Time Frames. When I am trading an account with $15,000 or more total equity, and if I've seen a consistent velocity trend with longer term support in the Strength Indicator Time Frames, I might not always pass up opening a new trade or close an existing one based on just a slight hesitation or move against my trustworthy trajectory in M1 and M5 time frames.

This is because I am personally willing to suffer a fairly big loss in order to ride out what I believe (at that time) is merely a retrace. Again, it's all based on the question as to whether or not I've seen a strong trend in the Foundational Time Frames AND alignment with velocity from the Strength Indicator Time Frames. If there is a visibly strong price movement trajectory, then I'll often ride out a retrace that might even extend into longer term time frames and add up to a fairly high number of pips. Again, it depends on how much of a loss you can sustain in order to ride out what looks like just a retrace in an otherwise strong trajectory movement.

Now, if a trader is working with only $1000 or less in an account, M1 and M5 are vital. You've got to make VERY fast decisions before opening your trade and after the trade is in play. You may be dealing with a Max Loss Rule of just 5 to 10 pips, so you have to get out if you see movement against you in M1 and certainly M5 (which is likely then showing sideways instability). Getting out of a trade with a small loss is not the end of the world. It's okay. You can absorb a small loss, especially if you're trading 1 lot or less. But with a small account, you must keep your eye on the M1 and M5 time frames to avoid the big loss.

I have heard of traders who keep the transaction window open to close out a trade and actually watch tick by tick when price movement gets close to the Max Loss Rule. That's starting to sound like "hoping" and "wishing" for the retrace to end, but it's okay. As long as you are willing to abide by your own Max Loss Rule, you'll be okay. Remember, we NEVER lose big. That is job one. That is an absolute you must keep in your mind at every moment. Never, never, never lose big. Of course, the definition of "big" varies depending on the size of your account. I hope that makes sense and doesn't sound contradictory.

TRAJECTORY WORKS EVEN DURING HOLIDAYS

2010.12.29 19:41	81.928	-4.13	2 470.46
2010.12.29 19:41	81.928	-4.13	2 450.93
2010.12.29 19:41	1.31824	17.04	5 240.00
2010.12.29 19:41	1.31824	17.04	5 240.00
2010.12.29 19:41	1.31824	17.04	5 240.00
2010.12.29 19:41	1.31824	17.04	5 240.00
2010.12.29 19:41	1.31824	17.04	5 320.00
2010.12.29 19:41	1.31824	17.04	5 240.00
2010.12.29 19:41	1.31824	17.04	5 296.00
2010.12.29 19:41	1.31824	17.04	5 296.00
2010.12.29 19:41	1.31824	17.04	5 296.00
2010.12.29 19:40	1.31824	17.04	5 296.00
2010.12.29 19:40	1.54603	0.00	3 256.00
2010.12.29 19:40	1.54603	0.00	3 248.00
2010.12.29 19:40	1.54603	0.00	3 192.00
2010.12.29 19:40	1.54603	0.00	3 128.00
2010.12.29 19:40	1.54603	0.00	3 016.00
2010.12.29 19:40	1.54603	0.00	3 144.00
2010.12.29 19:40	81.911	0.00	1 045.04
2010.12.29 19:40	81.911	0.00	1 132.94
2010.12.29 19:40	81.911	0.00	1 132.94
2010.12.29 19:40	81.911	0.00	1 093.87
2010.12.30 04:26	1.32411	51.13	4 576.00
2010.12.30 04:26	1.32411	51.13	4 536.00
2010.12.30 04:26	1.32411	51.13	4 536.00
2010.12.30 04:26	1.32411	51.13	4 536.00
2010.12.30 04:26	1.32409	51.13	4 520.00
2010.12.30 04:26	1.32409	51.13	4 520.00

2010.12.30 04:26	0.94220	-16.83	6 987.90
2010.12.30 04:25	0.94220	-16.83	6 987.90
2010.12.30 04:25	0.94220	-16.83	6 987.90
2010.12.30 04:25	0.94220	-16.83	6 987.90
2010.12.30 04:25	0.94220	-16.83	6 987.90
2010.12.30 04:25	0.94220	-16.83	6 987.90
2010.12.30 04:25	0.94220	-16.83	6 987.90
2010.12.30 04:25	0.94220	-16.83	6 987.90
2010.12.30 04:25	0.94220	-16.83	6 987.90
2010.12.30 04:25	0.94220	-16.83	6 987.90

8

Step By Step

Here is a very clear and concise step-by-step guide to Trajectory Forex trend identification as seen in several different scenarios.

1. You initiate the process of Trajectory Forex trend identification by looking at the Foundation Time Frames on a currency pair.

These are M15, M30 and H1 time frames. If you see a price movement trajectory that appears strong and consistent (even given the inevitable minor retraces in the opposite direction), then you likely have identified a current and active trend (or price movement trajectory). If you see price movement alignment in these three time frame charts and velocity is visible via a relatively high number of pips worth of movement compared to the collective retraces, then this is very possibly a trading opportunity and should be further investigated. You still need to look at the other Strength Indicator Time Frames in order to determine if this is nothing more than a scalping opportunity, or if you have long term alignment with velocity and a potential monster profit opportunity. There are no rules as to the exact number of pips that define a trustworthy trend. What's perhaps more important is observing a reasonably high number of total pips worth of movement that appears more consistent in direction versus movement up, down, up, down, sideways, etc. Obviously, more pips worth of movement one direction in less time is better. Higher velocity in price movement means greater probability of continued trajectory momentum.

2. If no consistent up or down price movement trend is visible in the M15, M30 and H1 time frames, then you should likely walk away for 6 to 24 hours. This is the typical daily routine I personally recommend where you scan through Foundation Time Frames on one currency pair after another searching for an opportunity. As well, NEVER underestimate the importance of Strength Indicator Time Frames to challenge what appear to be trends in Foundation Time Frames.

If you use the Foundation Time Frames to capture short term profits, always be aware of the level of risk involved. Take a look at the remarkable danger presented in the series of time frame charts below.

I call this the "Impending Doom" series. This shows us that identifying trends is important in the Foundation M15, M30 and H1 time frames, and we can certainly earn profits in the short term based on what you see here. But we must always be aware of the Foundational long term charts, because we may be looking at little more than a short term scalping opportunity.

It "looks" like there is a somewhat trustworthy trend trajectory upwards from M15, M30 and H1 Foundational Time Frames taken at the exact same time below.

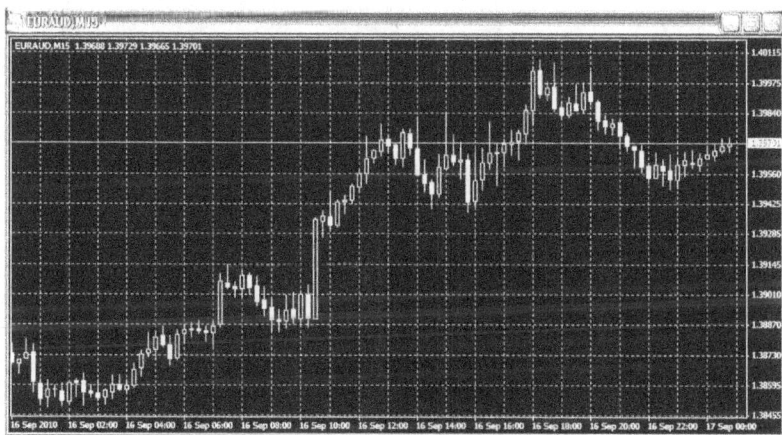

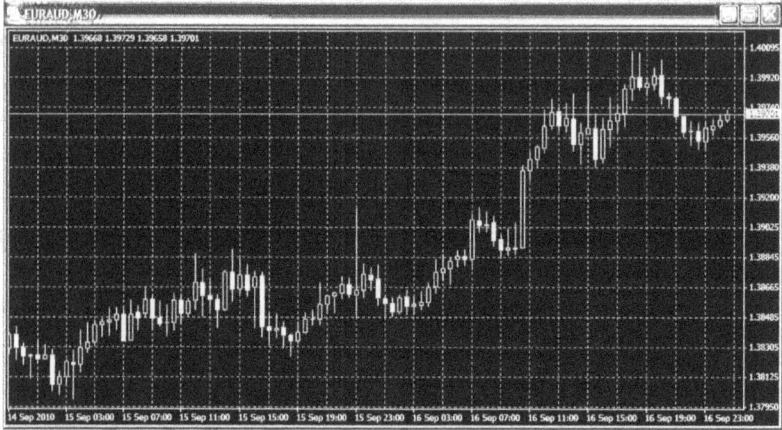

So far, you are feeling confident that you can BUY this currency and make a profit. In fact, I was bold on this day and I did, indeed, capture some hefty profits on a rising EUR/AUD scenario. But, look at the Strength Indicator time frames below and see the kind of risk I was getting into here. This was no safe bet, and definitely a short term profit taking opportunity only based on the data.

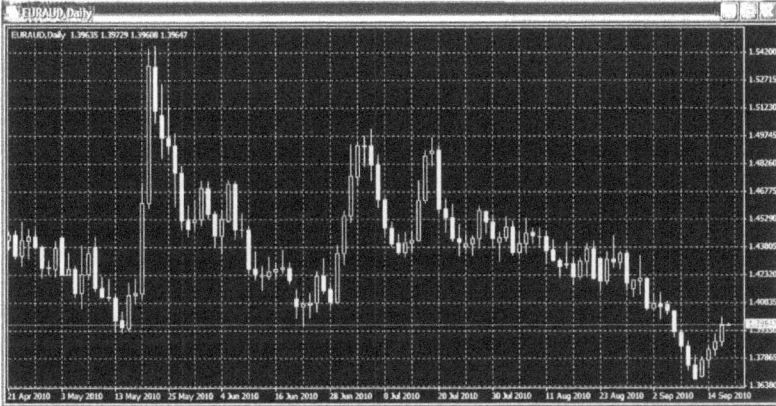

With a single click of the mouse, we see the Daily Strength Indicator Time Frame reveals that this currency is not in a strong, established upward trajectory. The Foundational M15, M30 and H1 charts were all moving in a trend direction that was AGAINST the longer term trend visible on the Daily Strength Indicator Time Frame.

So, we look at the next Strength Indicator, the Weekly Time Frame.

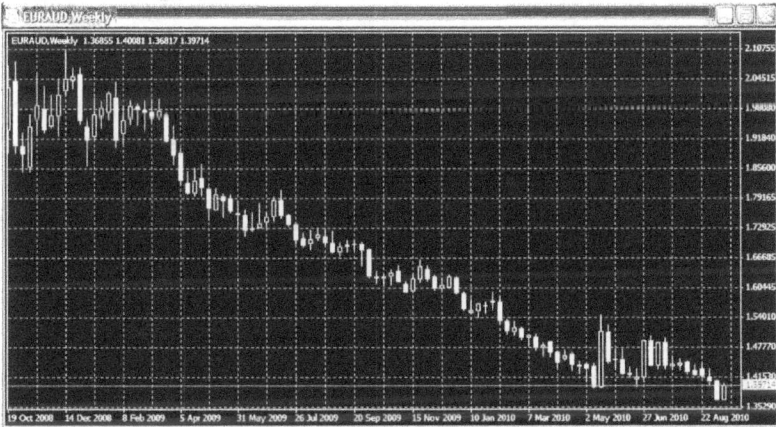

EUR/AUD here is in a free fall trajectory! The Foundational Time Frames are in strong disagreement with the Strength Indicator Time Frames to an incredibly high and strong number of pips worth of movement. So if we trade today based on the M15, M30 and H1, we will scalp only and not trust that upward movement. Let's still check the Monthly Strength Indicator out of curiosity.

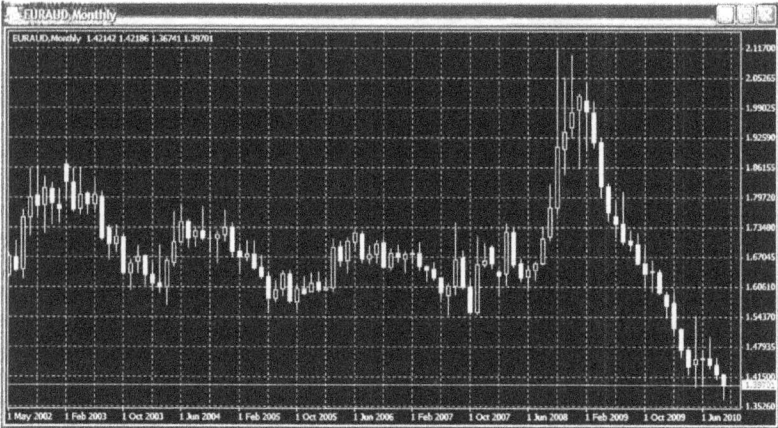

Okay. What we have here is a frequently seen scenario. There is Foundational Time Frame support for short term profit taking based on the M15, M30 and H1 time frames. So, yes, you can make profits EVEN when the longer term Strength Indicator Time Frames are in disagreement. You simply have to be very careful. The "gravity" or long term causal effect here is pretty strong, and it tells us that the Foundation Time Frames "may" be indicators of a change in the causal effect or overall trajectory, but we're not sure at this point. So, if we buy this pair today, we have a quick trigger finger. There is a causal effect pushing the price down with profoundly consistent velocity and it's been in place for a long time.

In the ideal scenario, you must always look for TRAJECTO-RY ALIGNMENT AND VELOCITY – where key time frames are aligned in the same price movement trend direction to a viable number of pips that reveal higher, consistent speed. Foundation Time Frames also remain important. You can make trading decisions based on M15, M30 and H1 trajectory, even though you have no long term Strength Indicator Time Frame support. You must simply be aware the absence of long term Strength Indicator support means less long term causal effect strength, only shorter term momentum if any is observed, and subsequent lower statistical probability that your trend will continue.

3. Below are M15, M30 and H1 Foundation Time Frames for EUR/USD at another point in time. You're going to see significantly strong upward movement. Take a look at these three charts and imagine this is what you see when you wake up one morning.

Okay. So you like what you see here, right? No doubt, you can make money today. No matter what you see in the Strength Indicator Time Frames, you can make money on this day, even if just scalping. There's strong upward Trajectory with sustained velocity. Total pips worth of upward movement, even in M15, far outpace total pips moved downward. This is high velocity, sustained movement upward. Now, it becomes a question as to how much trust you can put in the statistical probability that this trend of price movement will continue.

So, our next step is simple. As always, we must now look at the Strength Indicator Time Frames. We hope to see high velocity alignment, and we may already have an idea what we're going to find since we've likely been trading daily for a period of time, observing this pair (among others), and just WAITING to see the Foundation Time Frames align. Is this the case?

Outstanding. Our first H4 Strength Indicator Time Frame is in perfect alignment with the Foundational Time Frames, and the number of pips worth of movement reveals sustained and reasonably high velocity. This is looking good. This looks like a Trajectory with serious causal effects driving it upward. We may not know what's going on in the real world to cause it, but this looks good. So, let's look at the next Strength Indicator Time Frame.

Daily is good. A lot of pips moved in a shorter period of time. This is sustained speed. What's evidenced in the next Strength Indicator?

Wow. Weekly is in total alignment with high velocity pip movement as seen in every Foundation and Strength Indicator Time Frame so far. This is very, very good. This is a trend of great strength and consistent speed. Out of curiosity, let's look at the last Strength Indicator, the Monthly Time Frame below.

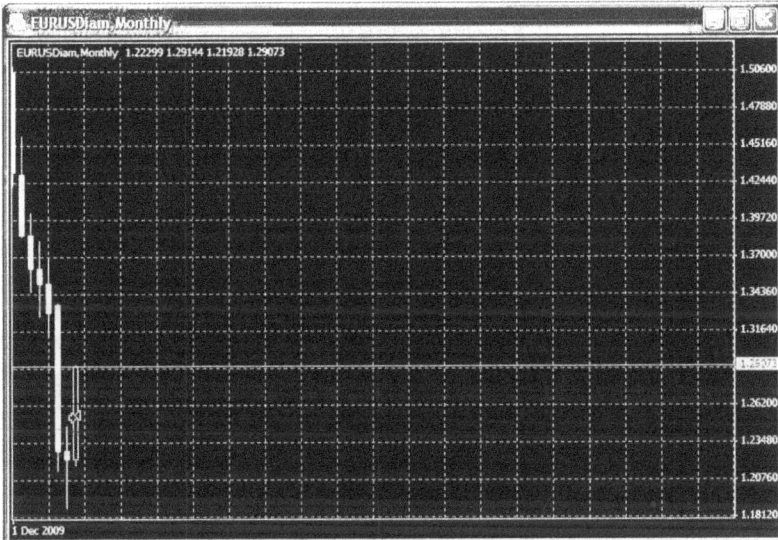

IT'S THE PERFECT STORM!

We've just found every single Foundation Time Frame showing an upward trajectory of great strength. M15, M30 and H1 all align perfectly in upward trend price movement with aggregate pips that reveal strong velocity.

Then, we have found the same 100% directional trend alignment and high velocity pip movement upwards in every single Strength Indicator Time Frame. H4, Daily, Weekly and Monthly all show the same strong upward trajectory.

What does this mean, if I even need to ask? We have a strong, strong trend. Price movement trajectory is going up. We only need to see M1 and M5 now if we're trading a small account under $1000 and we worry about the cost of minor retraces. Even in that case, when we catch an upward movement, we buy.

Since the trend of price movement is up here, you buy, buy, buy. As profits increase, even though you watch the occasional M1 and

M5 retraces that may threaten your Max Loss Rule, you add MORE lots in additional buys as the currency price continues upward trajectory. On a day like this one, you watch for profits to exceed your Max Loss Limit and then suspend the rule.

Now, instead of looking at possible escape based on the Max Loss Rule, you are soon only looking at how much of your profits you are willing to give back if things reverse significantly. So you will continue to watch M1 and M5, but likely just look for a major retrace or reverse to show up in M15. You should ride a strong trend like this one until it truly shows VERY strong signs of major retrace or reversal.

This one day can change your life depending on the size of account you start out with and how long you are willing to ride along with this trend. I was personally willing to endure a retrace that amounted to half my profits, because the Strength Indicator Time Frames were so strong and thus clearly revealed some massive causal effect driving upward movement. In the end, I captured hefty profits. Certainly, if nothing else, a single day like the one we've identified above can help you turn your small account into a major resource that significantly elevates your trading equity and profit potential.

I will tell you that this Perfect Storm scenario does not happen often. But being able to identify these strong trends is invaluable. No Technical Indicator or measure of Fundamental Analysis is as clear and obvious to read as these time frame charts. It's real time data, so you know you can trust it. Price movement and time frame data streams into your MT4 platform as 100% fact about the market's behavior. This is as real as it gets.

With Trajectory Forex as your trend identification methodology, you are also likely getting into trading opportunities like this one ahead of those pondering the nearly endless fortune telling chart patterns seen in Technical Analysis.

Are you starting to see how this works?

4. Now, let's focus on traders working with a relatively small account. Most new traders must start out with deposits under $1000. So, okay, you don't have a lot of free margin to absorb a big retrace.

After looking at the Foundation Time Frames (M15, M30 and H1), and THEN seeing confirmation of the trend in H4 and longer time frames above, you must still protect your small equity by looking at M1 and M5 as you make trades. In this case, you buy and start capturing profits, but you must pay attention to even small retraces in M1 and M5 because your Max Loss rule is going to be in play.

The Short Term Trading Time Frames are VERY important because they are the first indicators of trouble and a possible threat to your account. Always remember, the high leverage in forex means that big losses can add up just as rapidly as big profits.

So, for the smaller account trader, you must first look for Foundation Time Frame trajectory alignment with velocity (M15, M30 and H1), and also ideally look for Strength Indicator Time Frame trajectory alignment with velocity (H4, Daily, Weekly and Monthly). Equally important, you have to put great importance on observed, ongoing real time movement in the Short Term Trading Time Frames (M1 and M5).

In the below screen shots from the same Perfect Storm trend shown above, M1 and M5 time frames are in a slight retrace but that's because I could not capture the screen shots in time to show the upward movement. The thing to note here is that M1 and M5 time frames are showing STRONG overall upward movement, and we already know this is the SAME strong upward trajectory trend with velocity that we have already seen in Foundation and Strength Indicator Time Frames.

If we saw sideways movement or larger retracing in M1 and M5, perhaps we would wait to make trades. In this case, because of the strong and ongoing upward trajectory movement in the Short Term Trading Time Frames, we take our shot with the small account. All longer Time Frames show alignment velocity upward and we see ongoing upward movement in M1 and M5. This is worth the risk. So we make trades, and we still keep our finger close to the close trade button just in case the Max Loss Rule must be implemented. We are trusting Foundation and Strength Indicator Time Frames that support the ongoing upward trend trajectory we see in M1 and M5 Short Term

Trading Time Frames. Buy and see what happens, even though (as you see here below) small retracing is happening all the time. That's common in forex or any market. It's never a straight line. Just keep an eye on your Max Loss Rule and be calm.

M1 is strongly moving upward in alignment with Foundation and Strength Indicator Time Frames. The total number of pips worth of upward movement far exceed the retrace number of pips. Let's make money. Buy, buy, buy!

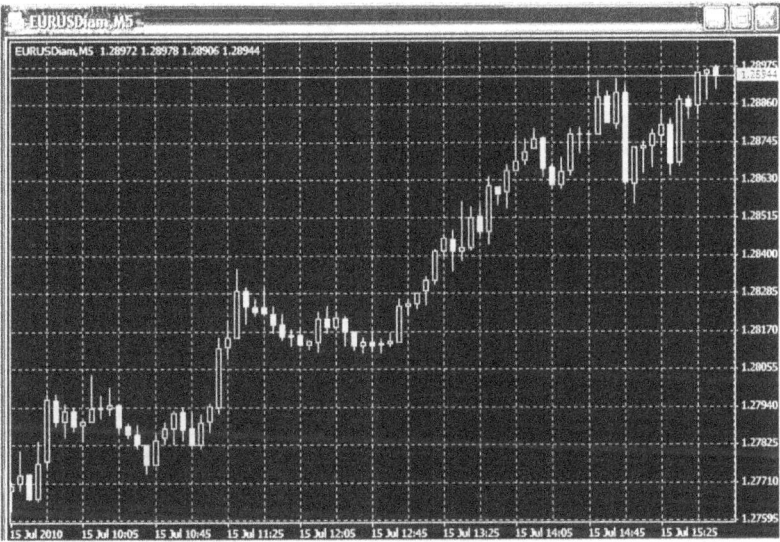

VERY IMPORTANT FOR THE SMALL TRADER!!! M5 agrees with the upward movement! Buy, buy, buy!

Okay, that's a great real time look and good advice. But, did this WORK? Here are screenshots of the time frames from later in the day that shows how you could have made money even with a small account and tight Max Loss Rule!

Okay. That's one afternoon. Here's the next day!

There was a continued trajectory trend price movement to a price level over 1.30030 from the initial screen shots at a price level of around 1.28980.

That's more than 100 pips of profit based on smart Trajectory price movement analysis.

This is a great example of sticking with a winning trade as long as you can stay awake. It is, however, also a great demonstration that all trends come to an end. As you can see in the charts from the next day above, the trend ended. For the small trader, that simply meant being well aware of what's going on and getting out before the profits you have earned are lost.

But, the big question is answered. Can you make serious profits with a small account and trading with a focus on short term movements? Yes! Should you pay attention to longer term time frame movements in the process? Absolutely! Trajectory Forex analysis works the same for small account traders as well as big equity traders.

5. We've looked at some successful scenarios so far. So what constitutes potential trouble? How do you identify those situations when you should STAY AWAY FROM MAKING ANY TRADES?

Let's look at another set of Time Frame Charts and observe price movement in all the key sets of time frames: Foundation, Strength Indicator, and Short Term Trading. You'll see below how Foundation Time Frames and Strength Indicator Time Frames "can" present what looks like a strong causal effect driving price movement in one direction, but M1 and M5 Short Term Trading Time Frames may actually signal trouble.

Here are the time frame charts showing price movement over various periods with GBP/CHF.

FOUNDATION TIME FRAMES (M15, M30 AND H1)

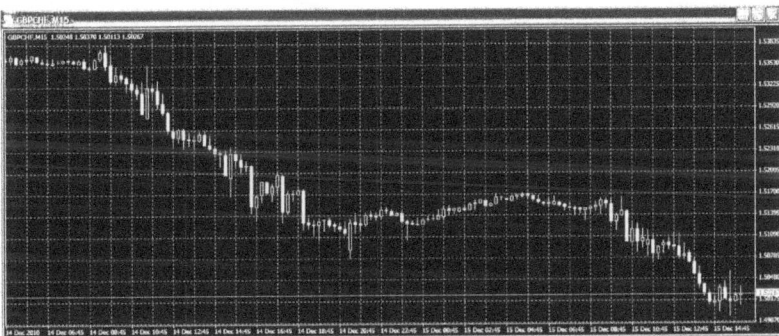

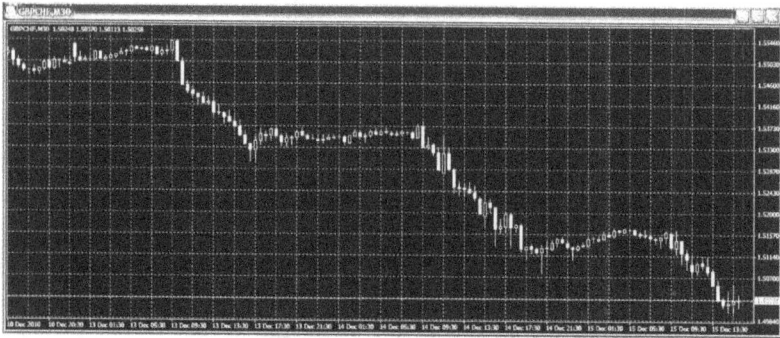

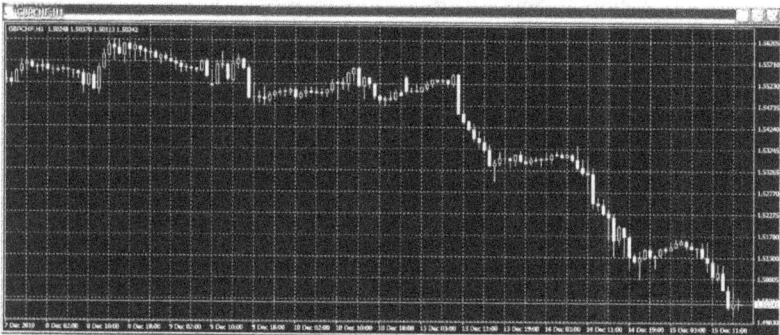

Price movement in the above set of time frames is definitely downward. There is, however, some sideways movement within the past few hours. Does this cause you concern or do you put faith in what appears to be a strong causal effect that's clearly driving the price down longer term? This price movement definitely "seems" to be very strong downward. Let's see what the Strength Indicator Time Frames tell us about the velocity of this downward price movement trajectory.

STRENGTH INDICATOR TIME FRAMES (H4, DAILY, WEEKLY, MONTHLY)

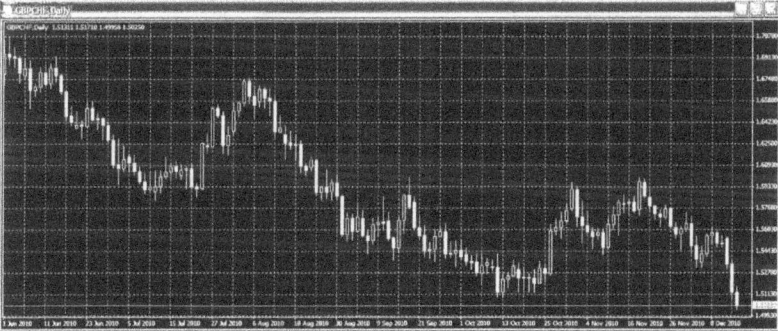

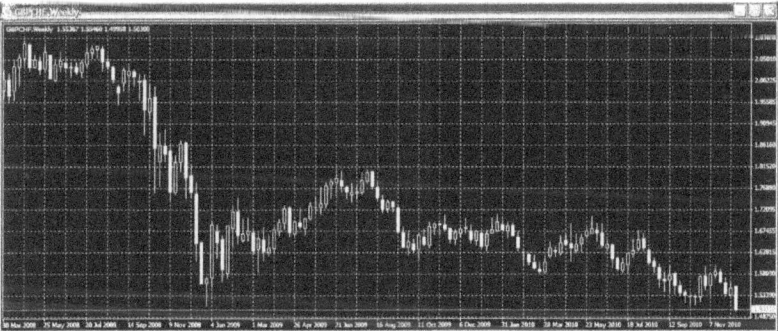

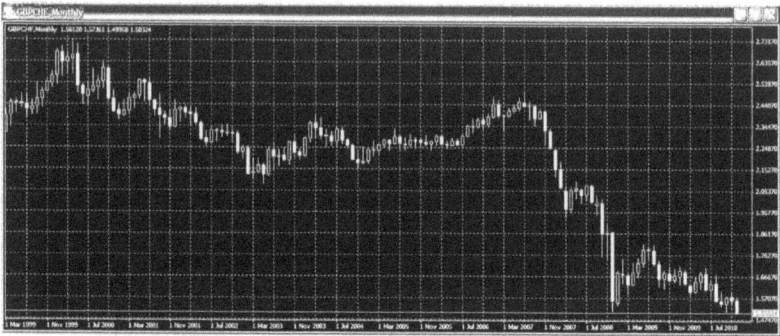

Foundation Time Frames (M15, M30 and H1) show the start of sideways movement. But, as we look at the long term Strength Indicator Time Frames, we see strong indication of some type of causal effect that is driving this price movement downward with relatively constant velocity. So, this becomes an interesting decision. Do we now sell this currency thinking it will resume consistent downward movement? Or do we wait? This "could" be a great opportunity to get into what looks like a strong and sustained downward price movement trajectory.

Before we open a trade, let's look at the M1 and M5 Short Term Trading Time Frames. To avoid possible trouble, let's look at what's happening NOW.

SHORT TERM TRADING TIME FRAMES (M1 AND M5)

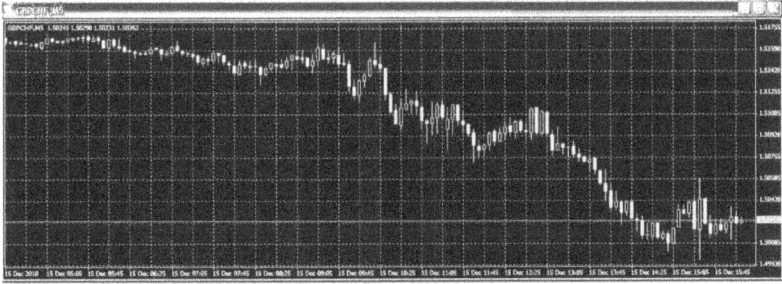

SIDEWAYS MOVEMENT IS CLEARLY THE DIRECTION AT THIS MOMENT.

Despite what appears to be a strong, long term downward trajectory movement, the currency has gone sideways for the moment. This is not a point in time to make a trade. You must wait. There's no value in "getting in early" on a trend. In fact, trying to "get in early" is usually going to cost you money. You only get into a trade when the time is right and that means trajectory with velocity is identified. Don't anticipate anything in forex. Trade In The Now with the real time data!

However, this is a very good currency pair to watch hour by hour based on the apparent causal effect that's driving price movement downward long term. It is most likely that the downward trajectory trend "should" continue. But, based on indications of sideways instability right now, we wait versus making a trade.

Here is the Foundation M15 chart just a few hours after the above charts. STILL UNDECIDED! Still sideways! We still make no trades even a few hours later. Downward movement has NOT resumed!

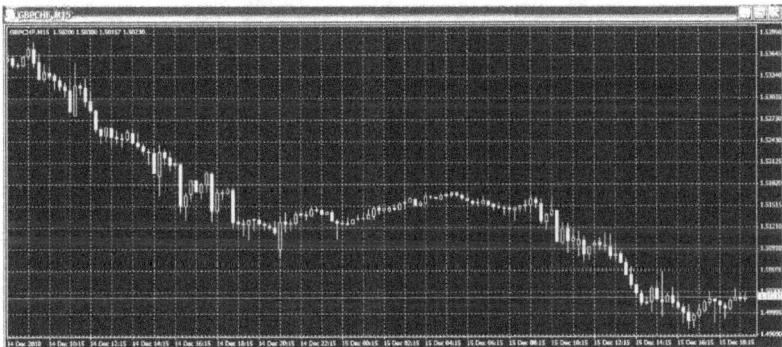

Now, here is the H1 time frame from the next day.

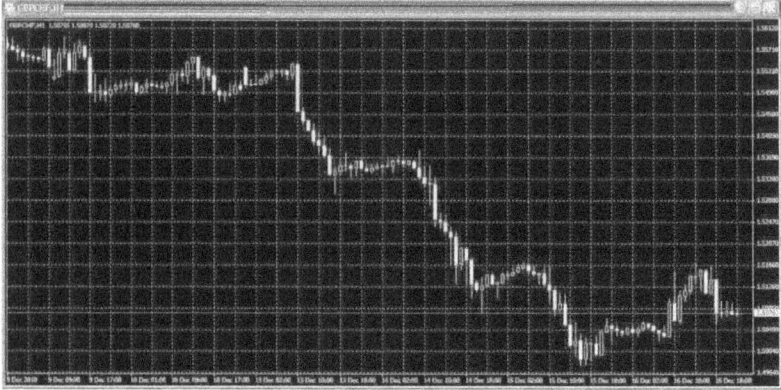

This is a roller coaster! We happened upon this currency pair at a point in time where Foundation and Strength Indicator Time Frames all showed us strong downward price movement. This looked like a solid trajectory that would likely resume, despite the initial indication of sideways movement. It looked like merely a temporary M1 and M5 retrace or what Multiple Time Frame Analysts would call insignificant noise in the middle of a powerful downward price movement trajectory. It very nearly looked like another Perfect Storm! Not so, and all the clues were there in the visible loss of velocity.

Instead, what we find about 36 hours later in the above H1 time frame is that the M1 and M5 sideways movement which HAD STARTED TO SHOW UP IN FOUNDATION TIME FRAMES (M15, M30 and H1) proved 100% true in revealing the loss of trend trajectory velocity!!!

This is another perfect example of the difference between Trajectory and Multiple Time Frame Analysis (MTFA) as discussed in an earlier chapter. If you were trading with MTFA, you would have likely just seen alignment downward, treated M1 and M5 as mere "noise" with no significance, and you'd have sold this currency. By the next day, your entire account might have been wiped out!

With Trajectory, we looked at the M1 and M5 time frames, observed a slowing in velocity, and determined that the sideways movement seen in the Short Term Trading Time Frames revealed a threat to the downward trajectory. This possible loss of sustained velocity seen in M1 and M5 was also hinted and confirmed in the small glitches starting to appear in M30 and H1 time frame movement. So, alignment alone does not reveal trading opportunities of any consistent reliability. We must always evaluate velocity of price movement in real time in order to determine the statistical probability of momentum and thus whether or not price movement will continue in the same direction.

Whatever causal effect drove this price movement downward for an extended period of time with high velocity had apparently started to lose its influence or another causal effect had come into play. Regardless of the real world reasons, we could clearly observe in this 100% true data that the price movement had started to go sideways. So, we made no trades and we made no mistakes. By the time we looked at the H1 chart over a day later (above), GBP/CHF had significantly retraced and continued sideways. There was no money to be made here with any level of confidence (despite the new upward movement that some might have contended was a profit opportunity). In truth, this was a HIGH RISK situation best avoided.

It was the "hint" of sideways movement just starting in the Foundation Time Frames and confirmation of continuing sideways movement in M1 and M5 that initially told us the trajectory velocity was weak. This is the perfect example of when you MUST avoid entering a trade, even though you could easily talk yourself into trading based on the long term downward movement or conventional Multiple Time Frame Analysis.

Always synthesize all the data. Always pay attention to what is happening right now. Do not rely on what's been happening in past hours, days or even weeks. You make money based on what happens NOW...not what happened even five minutes ago. The above sequence shows the importance of Trading In The Now.

In general, Short Term Trading Time Frames serve as the important first indicators of trajectory velocity deviation that can turn into costly trouble. As we've said before, our primary goal is to AVOID losses! So we don't want trouble and we don't want to get into questionable trades.

In the next scenario below, we're going to look at Short Term Trading Time Frames (M1 and M5) and again see that sideways movement is emerging. We are not going to bother looking at the Foundation or Strength Indicator Time Frames in this example, because it doesn't matter what they show given this short term data!

Even if you have what appears to be powerful up or downward trajectory movement, you CANNOT trust a trend trajectory when sideways movement emerges this strongly in both M1 and M5 Short Term Trading Time Frames. This is loss of velocity, and that means a threat to the ongoing trajectory.

If you have a trade open when you see this sideways movement appear, you must be prepared to get out quickly or possibly give back some of your profits to ride out what could become a hefty retrace or reverse. Sideways movement means instability evidenced by loss of velocity in the trend trajectory. Anything can happen next.

Here are two M1 and M5 time frames that reveal trouble in the form of unstable price movement trajectory in USD/JPY.

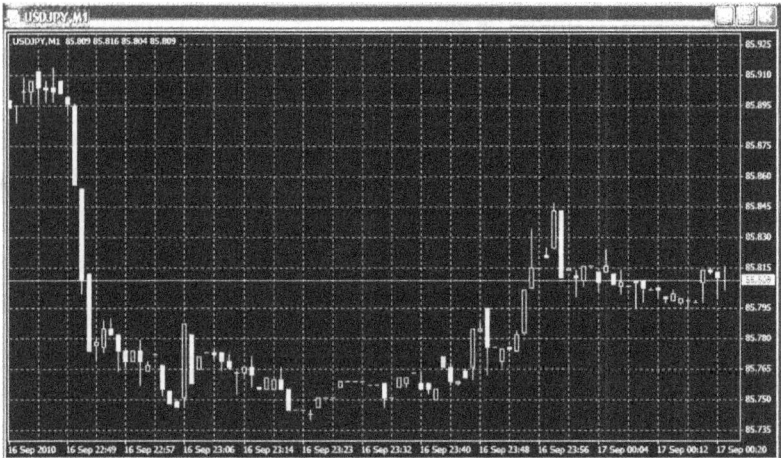

The M1 Time Frame here has clearly gone sideways. Let's look at M5.

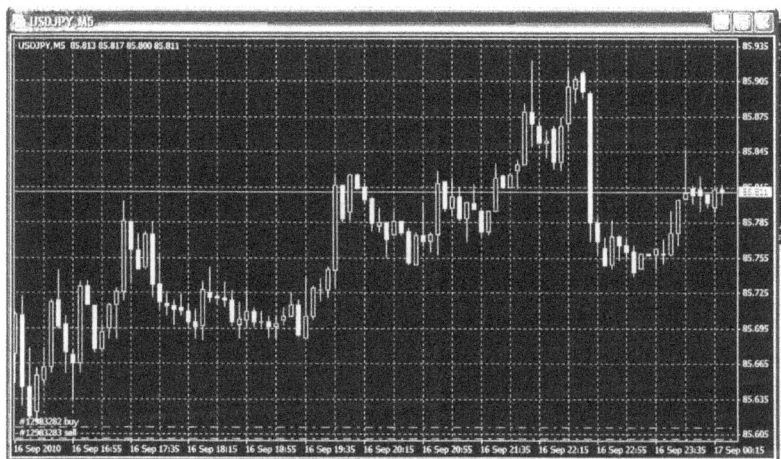

    This emergence of sideways movement or loss of trajectory ve-
locity means one thing for sure. There is instability and uncertainty
in the market. Notice the huge and sudden drop of price movement in
the last third of the above M5 time frame. Yet, that's not a downward
trend! The currency returns to sideways movement with no clear up
or down trajectory. This is a simple example of how quickly price
movement trajectory can move either direction during a sideways
stalled trajectory. A new trajectory with velocity may reveal itself in
coming minutes, hours or days. We can't predict the future. But we
know for certain we can lose money right now. Or, we can carefully
choose those moments when we can make money. We can Trade In
The Now based on real time data, and avoid price movement with
little to no upward or downward velocity.

    Think of sideways movement like an airplane climbing in alti-
tude. If it stalls, you could recover and continue your journey upwards.
Or, you could fall to the ground, suddenly just drop ten thousand feet,
or merely struggle along with little change in altitude up or down.
The question of up or down, however, is literally up in the air during
sideways movement which reveals loss of trend velocity. We have no
crystal ball, so we have no clue whether the "next" move will be up
or down. Do not trade with sideways price movement that reveals this
much loss of velocity in trajectory. This is high risk uncertainty!

The only time you might consider riding out sustained sideways movement is if you are ALREADY in a profitable trade, and you are willing to risk part of your profits (and your Max Loss Rule is not threatened). In this case, consider yourself a passenger sitting in the stalled airplane. You are not quite ready to jump out the door with a parachute in that first moment the plane stalls. You will, however, put your hand on the door knob and prepare to leap out!

Only in that situation would you consider waiting out an emerging sideways action to see what happens to the trajectory.

You "hope" the pilot can recover from the stall as the airplane hesitates in mid-air almost motionless. You "want" the pilot to recover and return to the airplane's upward trajectory. But you do not "know" what is going to happen to the trajectory of the plane in which you are sitting. Your life hangs in the balance, and if you value your money as much as I do, you probably treat it with the same gravity (pardon the pun).

So, yes, you can ride out sideways movement "if" Foundation and Strength Indicator Time Frames all align to support one strong, prolonged trend movement trajectory. But, you must watch the M1 and M5 time frames VERY closely. If you see sideways movement continue long enough to emerge in the M15 time frame, then it likely means your airplane is choking and struggling to maintain its current trajectory. Grab your parachute and get out of the trade. The probable outcome is not good when velocity is lost. Of course, if you have enough profits to ride it out, then you may remain seated in your stalled plane to see what happens. I will personally most often choose to pull the rip cord and pocket my profits. Later, should the trend resume, I will open a new trade. No worries. Again, I don't mind paying a small spread to the broker. It's a small price to be safely profitable. I will take my profits and catch the next plane.

Sideways trend movement is dangerous. It's showing you that the trajectory has become unstable. Momentum is being lost with every time frame that starts to reveal sideways swings up and down. Stay away from sideways price movement. Get out with your profitable trade, and do not get into a trade during sideways trajectory.

This should forever answer the question about a scenario some traders will occasionally identify as an acceptable time to trade based on misleading chart patterns, historical indicators or other signals. Regardless of prior activity, a stall in price movement velocity eliminates the opportunity to safely make profits. You should never open trades during sideways movement. You should also prepare to exit any active trades when sideways movement appears. Period.

6. You will identify more NO TRADE scenarios than SOLID TREND opportunities.

The unfortunate truth of the forex market (and actually any market you can trade on Earth) is that trends are simply not as strong, frequent or predictable as you would like them to be in order to make money every single day.

I can offer you, however, that attempting to identify trends with any other methodology besides Trajectory is foolish and invites serious financial losses. You can't trust Technical Analysis, because it relies on historical chart patterns to predict the future, and history does not repeat itself in the world of finance.

You can also choose to pursue your own interpretation of the latest Fundamental news, such as employment numbers, national debt, or whatever other things are going on in the world. This is foolish and naïve because you will not be able to perfectly synergize every piece of information that impacts prices, nor interpret exactly how all these pieces of information will have an impact in concert.

Some traders who first start to use Trajectory Forex tell me they get frustrated because they see so many situations where there are NOT trends according to the time frame scenarios I suggest are mandatory to align in substantial numbers of pips before revealing a legitimate profit taking opportunity. I simply respond that, okay, on that day you did not LOSE money!

That is a good thing. Because, when you do identify a solid trend, you have a higher statistical probability of making more than a few pips of profit that far outweigh even several small losses. Indeed, you can make 60 to 100 pips in a solid trend. That is a lot of money even at just 1 lot and 50 to 1 leverage. So it is worth your time to properly and conservatively identify a trend and escape mistakes with only small losses.

But, let's look at some time frame charts where you "might" think there's a trend, but the market is truly NOT trending. This next set of screen shots show a great "maybe" situation.

Please look over the following series of charts presented in the same order that I evaluated them myself, and let's see what conclusion you come up with as you look at the time frames. It's "close" to a trading opportunity. But see what you think.

First, you'll see the Foundation Time Frames (M15, M30 and H1). Second, you'll see the Strength Indicator Time Frames (H4, Daily, Weekly, Monthly). Third, you'll take a look at the Short Term Trading Time Frames (M1 and M5). Then, you have to make a decision to trade or not to trade.

Here's what you will wake up to on some mornings, and YOU will have to decide whether or not this is a profit taking trading opportunity.

FOUNDATION TIME FRAMES (M15, M30, H1)

Okay. At this point, you have mixed messages. It looks like we're seeing a downward trajectory and a pretty strong one. In the more recent period of time during this particular price movement trajectory, these Foundation Time Frames are showing either a strong retrace or the possible indication of a reverse. Is velocity lost? Is this just like the no trade scenario we saw in the previous section? How can we tell? Let's take step two in our Trajectory analytical process and look at the longer term Strength Indicator Time Frames.

STRENGTH INDICATOR TIME FRAMES (H4, Daily, Weekly, Monthly)

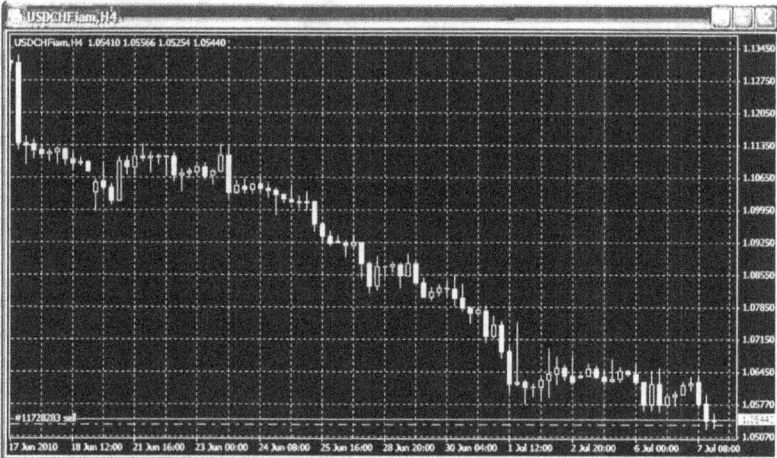

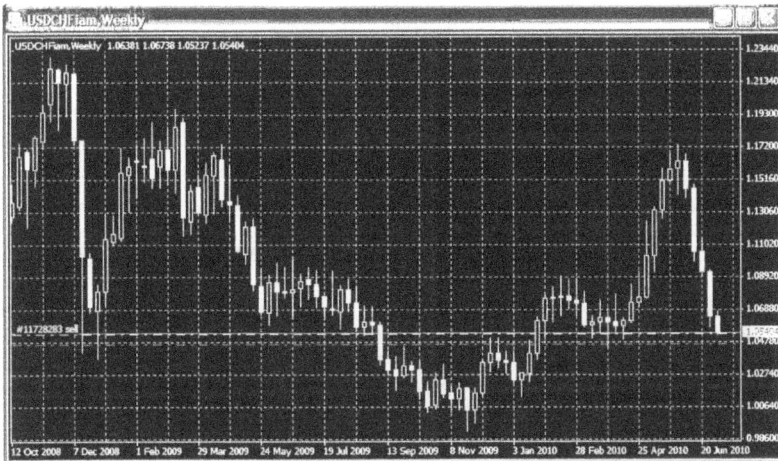

Well, these three charts seem to show a strong downward trajectory and create support for downward trending. What does the Monthly time frame show us? The last of our Strength Indicator Time Frames.

Now, this looks sideways based on the longest Monthly view in our Strength Indicator Time Frames. There have been some wild and potentially costly swings over the longer time period. So, this forces us to look back at Weekly, and we see something of a long term sideways trend if we go back a few months. Still, trending "looks"

downward right now, so there "looks" like a decent profit taking opportunity here.

While there is sideways movement that we are absolutely, positively supposed to avoid, let's just see if there's still a scalping opportunity in the Short Term Trading Time Frames despite everything we've learned so far. What's really happening in the now moment?\

SHORT TERM TRADING TIME FRAMES (M1 and M5)

Okay. Do you trade? The answer should be no.

There's a lot of indication in the Foundation Time Frames AND in the Strength Indicator Time Frames for a downward trend. But there are also some red flags. There's a serious loss of velocity here.

Despite the fact that I personally know many traders who will sit and stare only at the M1 time frame and try to scalp quick profits off only the short term moves, a simple examination of ALL the time frames to evaluate the "true" trajectory and velocity of price movement reveals problems with any trade at this time.

Now, I know you can see my own Sell trade on the last set of charts above. So, yes, I'm telling you one thing in terms of teaching but actually doing something else in my own trading. I was taking a risk I do not recommend for you at the initial stage of your learning process. I had a trade that was profitable at one point, and I ignored my own Max Loss Rule. That's ordinarily a stupid mistake. In the end, I made substantial profits on that sell trade, but only because I had enough equity to ride out the retrace. The risk was entirely too high and I should have captured my profits when they were there versus riding out the retrace. I based my decision to stick with that trade exclusively on the longer term sustained velocity behind that downward trajectory. I made a foolish decision to ride out what I calculated to be a higher probability of retrace versus reverse. I was correct...that time. But wouldn't it have been wiser to have simply captured small profits at the first indication of a major retrace, and then just opened a new trade AFTER the retrace ended and the trend resumed with velocity?

Even after several years, I still make mistakes. The fact that I ended up winning profits here is actually not important. I made a mistake. I should not have stayed in that trade when it retraced into a loss! There were more and bigger profits that would end up far out-weighing the loss if I had simply closed it out and waited for the next higher velocity move.

If you look at M1 and M5, there isn't enough velocity to merit a trade based on the overall sideways movement. So if you are Trading In The Now, you shouldn't even consider this an opportunity to scalp!

What is difficult about this set of time frames is that you "can" make a very strong case for trades if you isolate any one, two or three of the various time frame charts. Or, if you do as I did in this case, you can outsmart yourself analyzing the trajectory velocity long term versus short term, and find a way to convince yourself to make or stay in a trade mistakenly. It takes the entire perspective of every single time frame before you see the big picture of price movement trajectory and real time velocity.

More importantly, if there's a doubt, there is no doubt. This is unstable and likely in transition during the short term. Because of the instability in the M1 and M5 Short Term Trading Time Frames, you have no clue how many pips you may lose if you open a trade at this given moment. So loss of velocity and resulting fluctuations in price movement here can threaten your account equity thanks to the high leverage in forex. This is why it's a dangerous time to trade, despite the longer term movement in which I put my personal trust.

This is a great set of time frames where you may go back, look them over and say, "That's nuts. I see a trend here. I'm selling immediately." No doubt, selling this currency was a wise long term trade here. I did it myself successfully. BUT, with the high leverage of forex, do you really have enough free margin to cover what "could" be a significant retrace upwards? It all depends on your account equity and Max Loss Rule. And, why are you in such a rush to get into a trade? Why not wait for downward velocity to return?

Trading forex is first and foremost about NOT losing money! This is about certainty. This is about trying to shoot a hole in the argument that you can trust all the long term trajectory time frames and simply "ride out" a retrace.

NO ONE HAS ENOUGH EQUITY TO RIDE OUT EVERY RETRACE IN A HIGH LEVERAGE $3 TRILLION MARKET!

Can it be done if the retrace comes back to the trend before you run out of equity? Yes. I did it here. Do I advise that YOU do it right now? No. Don't take this kind of risk. Even I realize that I made a mistake here. But I also acknowledge that mistakes in forex are pretty common. You'll make them too. Sometimes you'll make a mistake and earn a profit. Other times it will cost you. The bigger lesson is to recognize your mistakes win or lose.

As you learn this Trajectory methodology for trend identification, you should look for what seem to be solid, consistent trajectory trends, but then search for indications that it truly is NOT trending. Look for possible indications that there "could" be a problem with the trend. Is the trajectory of price movement changing? Is the velocity slowing down or going sideways? If so, there "could" be a costly retrace or even a reverse.

That may sound negative, but you must constantly battle the human optimism that lives in all of us. We all "want" to see a trend. We all "hope" we wake up in the morning and there's a big profit opportunity staring at us in the time frame charts. We all want a profitable trade to become MORE profitable.

Hopes and wishes should not be part of your support for a trading decision, even if you know how weak the USD is in relationship to the CHF (as shown in the above charts).

You will not make money today based on what happened yesterday. You will make money based on what is happening right now. With rare exception, the trader reading this book cannot sustain the losses that "could" happen during retraces that can transpire between today and tomorrow.

I urge you to use the following rule: If there is a doubt, there is no doubt. That applies to situations where you do not trade just as it applies to scenarios where you seriously go for it. What you will find, as you learn and trade with Trajectory over months and years, is that your ability to trade free of doubt will greatly increase. Your confidence and ability to "see" the probabilities will increase with every passing day. Trajectory requires you to make qualitative decisions on statistical probability based on quantitative data. Practice will give you the ability to make better, more confident decisions with each passing day.

7. Are there times when you should "seem" to break the rules? Absolutely.

There is a clear discipline behind Trajectory trend identification. At the same time, it is not so rigid that we can make absolute rules (despite my every effort to give you some serious guiding principles).

You will often find yourself smartly selecting isolated time frames and making decisions that lead to profitable trades right in the face of dangerous sideways movement or an absence of strength indicators for the trajectory you want to trade. It is sometimes okay, for example, to trust an alignment of just H1, M30, M15, and M5. You may also, as I did in the previous example, invest great faith (and money) in the longer term strength of trajectory and velocity as seen in H4, Daily, Weekly and Monthly.

This is profit taking based on solid information that YOU must analyze! Your goal is to look over the collective data and not only see the trajectory of price movement, but evaluate its strength via observing velocity of price movement. This is about looking at quantitative data that's 100% true, but you must ultimately use this 100% true, real time data to make qualitative decisions about statistical probabilities.

There are profit taking opportunities that show up all the time and you will NOT see perfect alignment or consistent high numbers of pip movement to identify trustworthy velocity behind the observed trajectory. Indeed, you will likely see more situations where things are far less than perfect versus coming across those moments when you catch the "Perfect Storm" alignment of substantial trajectory movement across all time frames.

The perfect alignment is rare, so you must learn to quickly profit on scenarios like these below.

There is a clear trajectory and visible velocity of price movement. This is a solid opportunity to sell the EUR/USD and make profits here. Movement is strong in short term through H1. So, clearly, based on the above series of time frames, you SELL the currency and make profits!

These charts show an immediate opportunity. Do you pass it up? You can't or you will go weeks without making a trade. So you make the trade. You Trade In The Now.

But, you must have a QUICK trigger finger in the event you need to get out of the trade if it turns against you.

Below is the ominous H4 Strength Indicator Time Frame taken at the exact same time as the above screen shots.

The H4 time frame screen shot below shows the longer term trend is SIDEWAYS and actually UPWARDS (and this longer term UPWARDS trend is confirmed in Daily, Weekly, and Monthly time frames). LONG TERM SUPPORT IS NOT HERE. BUT, this is STILL a profit opportunity if you are willing to take a little risk and get in and out of the trade fast.

H4 below simply gives you a clear warning this is not a STRONG trend. You must make your profits now in MINUTES, not HOURS, and be prepared to get out quickly if the currency price movement turns against you in M1 and M5!

Here is the chart that tells you this is ONLY a short term profit trend trajectory. Note the longer term UPWARD and SIDEWAYS velocity of movement? This is a big time warning that there's some kind of causal effect driving EUR/USD upward, so your short term SELL will last only a brief period. But you CAN make money.

Again, this is where your judgment in utilizing this methodology is important. Please note that this is NOT "guessing". This is kind of like kicking a football 60 yards down the field and yet you can CLEARLY see a hurricane is approaching right in your face! You KNOW the wind is going to pick up fast and blast the football back toward you, but you ALSO know the wind is calm right now and the football is still going rapidly downfield after about 30 yards. Will it make it a full 60 yards before the wind changes and that hurricane hits the ball?

This is why you must look at M1 and M5 charts during this kind of short term profit opportunity. A strong wind gust ahead of the storm could hit at any moment. Equally important, the storm is NOT on top of you and things look promising for the ball to continue on its current trajectory for a fair distance.

The price movement trajectory is simply "threatened" by long term trend movement in the H4 and longer time frames.

This emphasizes the importance and value of looking at real time data that we know to be 100% true and then making smart determinations of statistical probability relative to continued price movement as it is happening before your eyes in the time frame charts.

This above scenario is very common. You CAN make profits when several time frames align to show you strong, reasonable numbers of pips worth of movement in one direction.

This definitely is a trend with short term trajectory velocity! It's simply not a strong or long term trend. That's the key. There is clear price movement trajectory downward. Velocity is simply not supported in longer term time frames, because the long term trajectory is actually upwards.

This brings us back to the discussion of statistical probability. We can still make profits even when the statistical probability of a long term trend is weak. Indeed, MOST of your profits will be made with less than perfect scenarios, which means you have to evaluate the statistical probabilities.

Here's another example of a profitable trade when conditions are not perfect. It's characteristic of MOST profit taking situations you will identify. The trade I opened here is visible at the bottom of each time frame chart. Watch the numbers change in the trade at the bottom of each frame. This is a live trade as it happened, so you can watch as my profits grow based on my own analysis of the real time data in this instance.

Foundation Time Frames

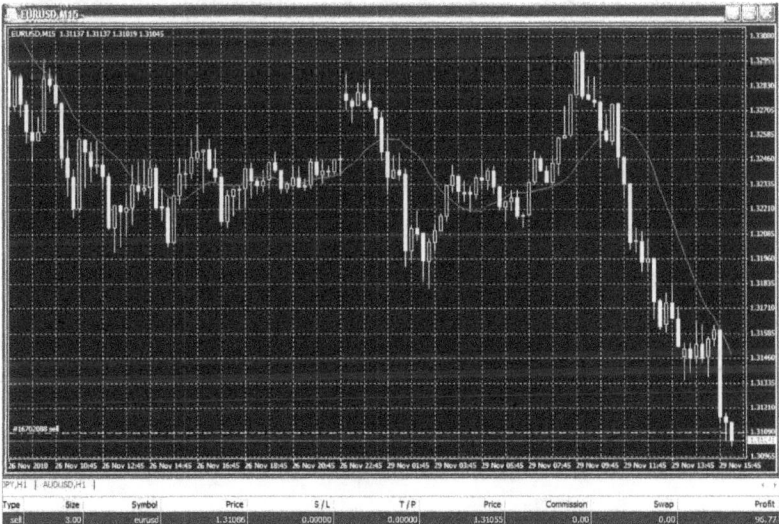

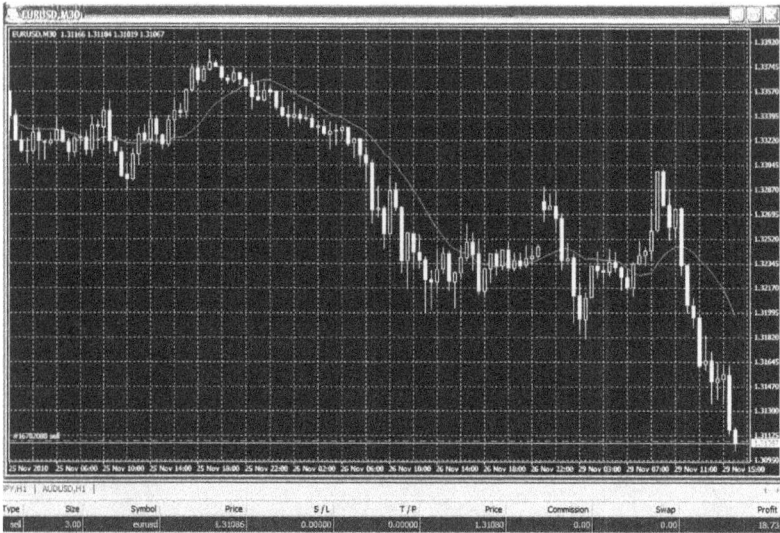

The Foundation Time Frames show a strong downward trend trajectory. I'm making money.

Strength Indicator Time Frames

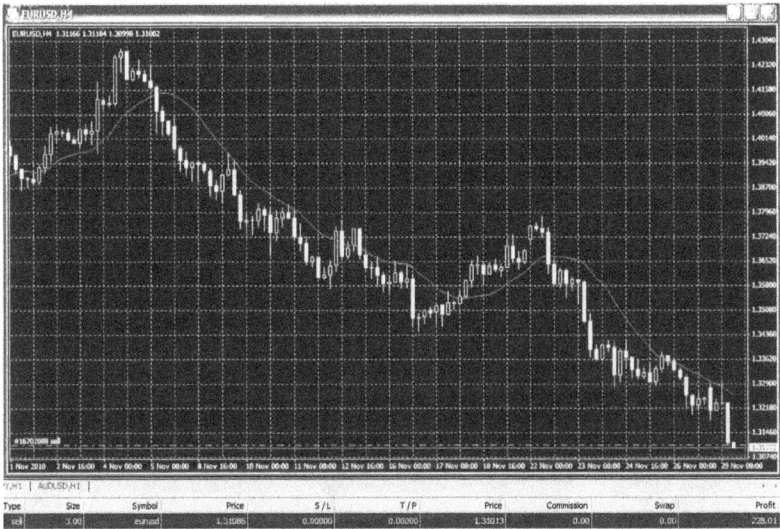

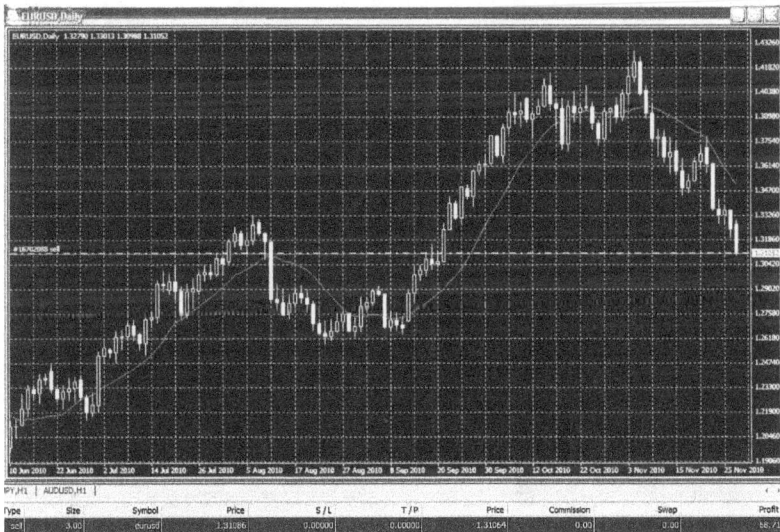

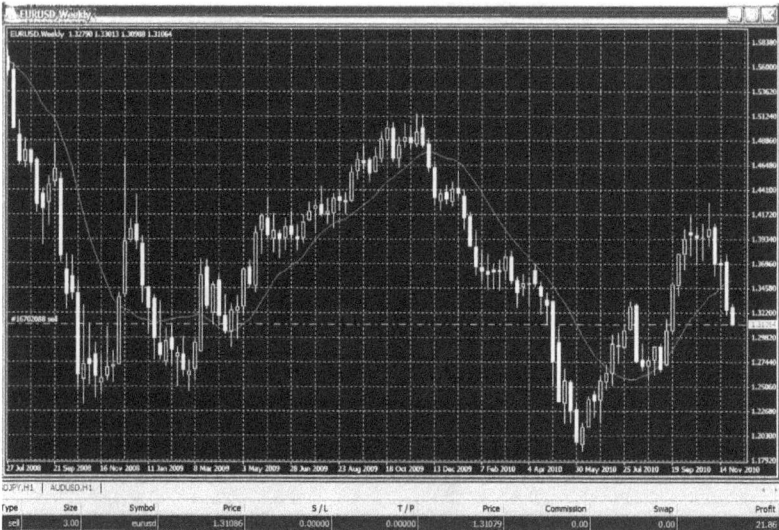

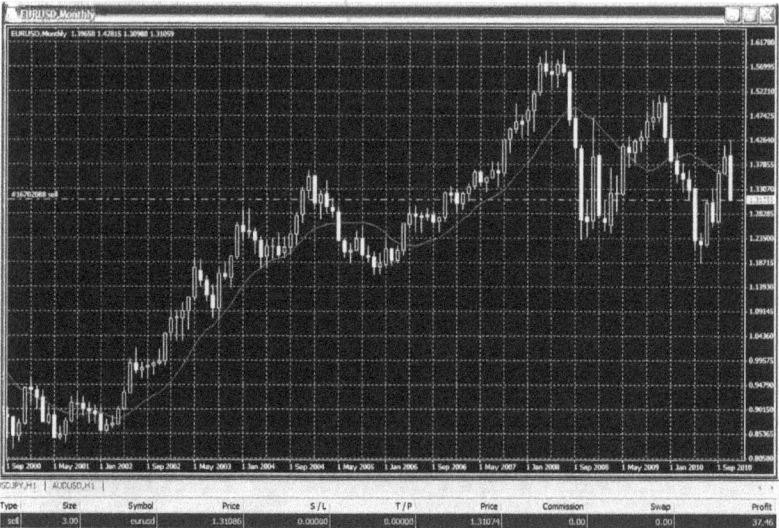

The longer term Strength Indicator Time Frames above show this downward trajectory is not as strong as it appears in the Foundation Time Frames. Indeed, this is a long term sideways or upward direction that could change against me at any moment during my sell trade. There is, however, definitely enough real time downward movement with velocity to trade for profits based on the above data.

Did we make profits on this shorter term trend? Yes. As you can see from the fluctuations in profit at the bottom of each chart, it's a trade with relatively low statistical probability of continuation. But, this is a great example of Trading In The Now and aggressively capturing profits on a short term trending trajectory.

The entire time we sit here with an open trade, we must be aware that getting out with only a small loss at worse is essential since we have been aggressive and made a three lot trade. So what happened? Did it retrace and force us to get out? Did it continue and produce profits?

Here are the subsequent profits shown in the Short Term Trading Time Frames.

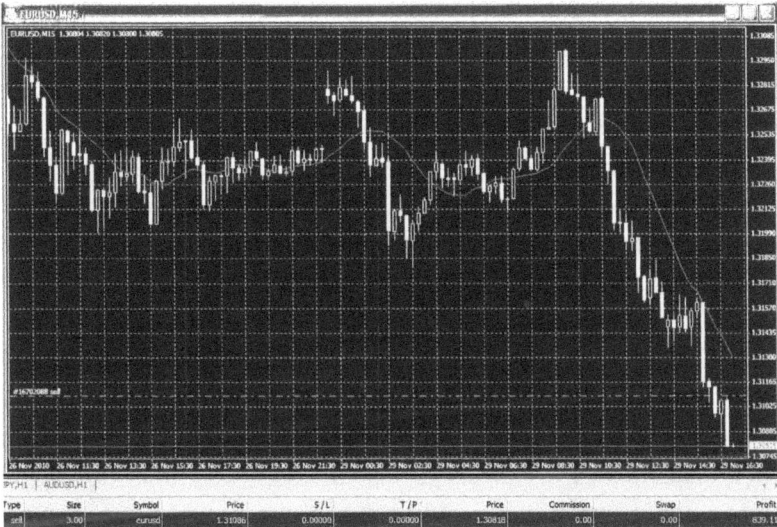

Now, the trend actually continued to a profit level over $1000, but I stayed with the trade until it retraced and delivered a final profit to me of about $800. That's when I closed the trade and watched the currency's movement for possible added profit opportunities. Remember, at the time, this was a downward trajectory that contradicted longer term Strength Indicator Time Frames. My confidence was not high that it would continue. The data indicated a lower statistical probability of this trend continuing for any length of time. So, getting out fast and profitably was the wise move. But, did the trend continue further downward?

Below is the return to sideways movement over the next several hours that we feel, at this time, legitimately identified the end of that short term trend. It's important to note that, even with long term Strength Indicator Time Frames showing little to no support for this downward trajectory trend, there might still be a great profit opportunity yet to be revealed in the real time data. Maybe.

This is a great example of how statistical probability works. I opened a profitable trade, in this case, knowing from the start that there was likely just short term velocity and thus a marginal statistical probability of continued movement in the same trajectory trend direction.

I made my profit and I closed the trade. But what should you do next?

On the trade shown above, I made the sell you have already observed with a quick trigger finger and willing to get out with a small loss if it immediately retraced (which could have happened). Fortunately, like most trades of this type, the trend did not end at the exact moment I jumped in. It continued for a brief time and I earned a reasonable net profit by getting out after a brief retrace at the $800 to $1000 profit level.

This is the most typical trade you will make via the Trajectory Forex methodology. Below is the end of this short, temporary, weak but highly profitable trend. Or is it? At the time of taking this screen shot, I had no idea.

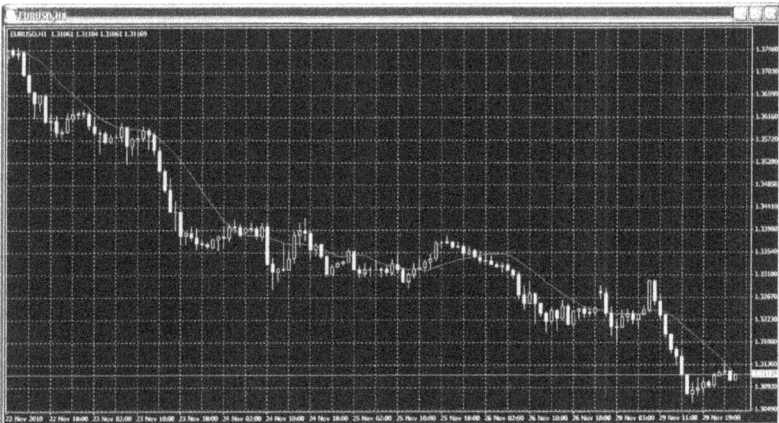

After what seems to be just a short term trajectory trend profit opportunity, and then significant sideways movement which we know to be dangerous, we must still watch to see if the initial trend on which we just capitalized resumes on the same trajectory with velocity. It is not uncommon for one profitable trade to be followed closely by ANOTHER profit opportunity. Simply continue to Trade In The Now!

We always have to figure that there was some "causal effect" that prompted that sudden downward movement. If so, MORE profits could be earned "if" that same trajectory trend resumed. What happened here?

While the trending trajectory seemed to end by the end of the U.S. trading day with a major and sustained sideways move, we had to continue to watch and see what might happen next. Would the trend resume after a period of sideways movement, and perhaps gain even more strength?

The reason a resumption of the same trend might have more strength is because there is now clearly some "causal effect" that's continuing to drive this trajectory trend price movement. If you see ANOTHER downward movement, then you're possibly recognizing that the real time data is revealing a continuing and building velocity behind this recent downward trajectory. If that begins to happen with any solid strength (faster versus slower price movement downward in this case), then you should jump on top of the renewed trend and see what happens. Sell and watch.

As the below chart shows, I waited patiently, and (even though the price was still inside the sideways movement range at the time I entered the below trade), I finally saw a fast and strong move downward which triggered my own move to get in with a big sell trade of six lots. I simply watched for some serious SPEED of that first downward movement as revealed in M1 and M5, and then I felt it was worth a shot to open another sell trade.

With the rapid downward movement, profits added up quickly. It was clear that the data was showing something driving this price downward...a causal effect revealed ONLY by the data in real time! This is the very definition of Trading In The Now!

End result? I stayed with it, even through a period of strong retrace because I was already willing to give back half the profits. (Remember, after we achieve profitability, we CAN suspend our Max Loss Rule because we are risking profits...not our core equity.)

The result of this patient Trajectory analysis was the hefty profit shown below of just under $8000 in less than 12 hours.

Type	Size	Symbol	Price	S / L	T / P	Price	Commission	Swap	Profit
sell	6.00	eurusd	1.31183	0.00000	0.00000	1.29916	0.00	0.00	7 936.86

There are some critical lessons in the above example.

Don't hesitate to seek profit taking opportunities in what are openly identified as likely short term trends. If all time frames don't agree, that's fine. All you really need is Foundation Time Frame velocity and alignment, and then keep an eye on M1 and M5 so you don't lose money quickly.

If M1 and M5 show some measure of velocity and the same trajectory as the Foundation Time Frames, then there's likely a short term profit opportunity in front of you and you should open a trade to capture even just a few pips worth of profit. But stay with the trend until it goes sideways in M15, hits your Max Loss Rule, or threatens a third to half of your net profits after any reasonably successful run.

It's also perfectly fine to simply capture four or five pips worth of profit and close the trade. But always watch for continued price movement in the same direction after you exit a trade, and be ready to open a new trade on a continuing trend. As long as you're making more than you're losing, it's a good way to go until you feel more comfortable trusting the data.

As you saw in the above example, always continue to watch a profitable trend trajectory even after it goes sideways. You know there was some reason for the initial trend movement...a causal effect.

So, if price movement returns to the same trend trajectory, you are likely safe and smart to jump on it because an increase or resumption of price movement velocity should give you confidence in the trajectory of movement. Trade and realize you NOW have a trend trajectory that is growing in strength. Again, we don't have long term support, but the trend is happening before your eyes. So take profits when the opportunity presents itself.

This is the importance of working with real time data. You make real time decisions based on what's happening at that moment. Trade In The Now, and you will likely profit. Trust the data and act in the moment.

Also, as an additional note, keep a demo account active in order to challenge yourself on days when you turn down a trading opportunity with your live account. More often than not, you will find yourself making more aggressive and successful trades in the demo account based on the data (but sometimes seemingly risky), and you will build your knowledge and confidence in this Trajectory Forex methodology focused entirely on data-based trading.

You'll also learn more about getting out of losing trades quickly, and easily absorbing the small loss that you can make up on the next trade. Proving this to yourself in a demo account, where you are likely to take seemingly greater chances versus letting the emotions of money at risk take over is important.

Your emotional and logical trust in the data is hard won, but essential. You must get to the point where you realize you are, in fact, never really taking "chances". You are always making intelligent decisions based on your interpretation of factual data that's 100% true in real time as it streams into your trading platform. This is not guessing. This is not speculating. This is not predicting. This is analyzing statistical probabilities based on data. This is Trading In The Now based on your interpretation of observed fact. Your ability to make accurate, high confidence decisions will grow with each passing day.

Also remember, you don't have to make big total pips in every trade. If you make 5 trades in a day that yield net profits of just 5 to 10 pips each, then you've had a very profitable trading day. Again, avoid big losses and always focus on putting net profits into your account at the end of each trading session. That's the key to turning this from a hobby into your profession…consistent profits. No big losses.

8. Causal Effect. How does it impact my decisions? It is important to know that the statistical probabilities revealed by Trajectory Forex represent causal effects. We are identifying "something" that is happening in the real world. So trending price movement represents something real happening that has an impact on currency values.

Whatever we are seeing in the data is identifying some causal effect in the real world that could be anything from a supply/demand dynamic to a major world event. There is always a reason the price is moving in one direction or another, and this is what the Trajectory data reveals (even though we may not know "what" the causal effect is at any point in time).

If the price is going sideways, the loss of velocity means instability and uncertainty. There might be no significant causal effect behind these currency values, or (more likely) myriad causal effects are canceling each other out in terms of impact on price.

If there is a trend, and it hesitates but then resumes with a higher velocity of movement, then there is likely some nature of strong causal effect that is the reason behind the trend resuming in the same direction. You don't need to know what the real world causal effect is…it doesn't matter. You just need to know that price movement is not arbitrary.

This is why sideways movement is so dangerous. Sideways movement is the indication of indecision in the market, and instability you cannot trust. Think of it as if the price is just waiting for some minor causal effect to take place and send it shooting off in any direction. Sideways movement is just brutally unstable.

You should typically not trade when you see sustained sideways movement in the Foundation Time Frames, H1 and below. You should likely also not open new trades if you see sideways movement sustained in Short Term Trading M1 and M5 time frames. Obviously, this same sideways movement in M1 and M5 is also a threat to any open trades. So watch carefully and have a quick trigger finger ready to escape when the velocity behind a trajectory is lost.

Sit back, watch, and wait out strong, sustained sideways movement. It indicates that the market itself is waiting for some causal effect to reveal itself.

This can't be predicted. It can only be observed in real time as it happens!

If you learn any single thing from this system, I hope you gain a true appreciation for how absolutely absurd it is to attempt to "predict" price movement via Technical Analysis. Historical chart patterns have nothing to do with the future movement of currency prices. Currency prices move based on financial events that are happening in the now. No "historical" chart pattern, spinning tops, channels or other past indicators can consistently "predict" what is going to happen in the future.

What's worse, almost every major broker in the world teaches new traders that Technical Analysis is the key to making money in forex. It's absolutely not true. The novice trader cannot master Technical Analysis. More significantly, even professional technical traders openly admit that they make money via money management and win, at best, only 40% of all trades! Technical Analysis is the biggest reason 80% of all new traders in forex lose all their money.

So clear your mind, be objective, and trust only the 100% true real time data that reveals the true Trajectory of price movement.

9. The Max Loss Rule Is Mandatory! Let's say you have a relatively small account, or you're not yet confident in your ability to identify trends via Trajectory Forex. This is a time when you need a tight Max Loss Rule like 5 pips. What does this mean? It means that you close out your trade when you lose 5 pips no matter what the time frames look like, and disregarding the "possible" or seemingly "inevitable" move in your favor that "should" happen.

No matter how confident you feel that the price movement is going to ultimately trend in your favor, if you hit your Max Loss Rule, get out of the trade with the small loss. NEVER LOSE BIG!!!

Now, after closing that trade with a small loss, you don't just walk away defeated. You should stay at your computer and watch to see if the trend in which you initially placed so much confidence actually resumes. In most cases, you have likely identified the trend correctly, but you've cut your losses by getting out according to your Max Loss Rule. That's okay.

When the trend resumes, you will jump back into it with a new trade and make your profits. If the trend is real, then you'll have new confidence and likely make more pips than you lost. At the worst, you should break even. Regardless, winning a small profit is better than taking a net loss at the end of the day. So accepting a small loss should do nothing but motivate you to be more active. Scan through more currency pairs looking for trend scenarios in the time frame charts. Make more trades.

Never worry about the cost of the spread. The more you trade, the more you will capture significantly more pips than you lose. The key is that you never lose big! Losing big is disaster. Losing big is unacceptable.

Never lose big. Never.

10. If your winning trade continues for a fair number of pips worth of profit, and your trade is up, stay with it. After 10 – 20 pips profit, you may use something like a "One Half Loss Rule".

There is an interesting dynamic that makes no sense, but I hear it from one trader after another. "I had made 22 pips profit, so I got out because I just KNEW there was big trouble when I saw a 6 pip retrace." It makes no sense when people tell me this because they were still up 16 pips profit. Yet, I hear about this type of panic escape from a profitable trade all the time.

Routinely and unfortunately, the next sentence I often hear is, "And it was a shame I got out, because the retrace ended and it came back another 14 pips the same direction in just a couple minutes. If only I had stayed in that trade!"

Please, when you are riding a trend and it is moving in your profitable trend trajectory, stay in the trade and make money until it seriously retraces or reverses. My rule is One Half or One Third Loss of Profit and then I'll get out.

If you are riding a trend moving in your direction, then the more profit pips it moves…the more pips you can risk that the trend will continue.

Let's suppose you correctly identify a Trajectory price movement trend and you make a buy or sell trade. After 30 minutes, you've made 25 pips worth of profit. But then there is a retrace of 5 pips. Uh oh. 5 pips was your maximum loss rule! So what do you do?

I advise that you are already up by 25 pips, so now you have suddenly dropped back to a 20 pip profitable position. You "could" get out according to your Max Loss Rule, and see what happens, but now – after a total of 25 pips movement on top of whatever number of pips worth of movement you observed when you first identified the Trajectory, a 5 pip retrace is not a concern as long as you see a quick return to the continued Trajectory trend movement in M1 and M5 Short Term Trading Time Frames, or sideways movement that is relatively small in terms of total pip movement and brief in terms of time.

Indeed, if I have personally made 25 pips of profit on a trade with strong velocity of movement in the same trajectory, then I am willing to give back a full third to half of those pips (or up to about 12 pips) in order to see if the trend will resume. Price movement trajectory with short, mid and long term support in time frames is worth trusting. Be aggressive. But yes, also be smart.

The other acceptable approach is to simply capture your profits and wait for the trend to resume, especially considering that the average spread will be only about one pip. It's a small price to pay in order to put those profits in the bank. So, you should trust your own judgment as to whether you ride out a retrace or jump out of a trade in order to capture profits. As you implement this Trajectory methodology over a longer period of time, you will grow much stronger in your ability to identify those situations where it's safe to ride out a retrace.

It's all about your ability to observe fluctuations in price movement velocity and make accurate qualitative decisions about the probability of continued trend movement based on the streaming real time quantitative data.

Of course, all good things come to an end. This means all Trajectory trends come to an end.

When you see sideways or reverse movement in the M15 chart for any period of time, then you can and should likely move on to another currency or just walk away with money in the bank.

It is truly impossible for me to give you absolute rules. The combinations of trajectory trending price movements at different velocities of total pips in various time frames are practically endless. Thus, the key skill is using this quantitative, 100% true real time streaming data to make qualitative trading decisions based on statistical probability.

Here is my best suggestion on how to further elevate your statistical probabilities of winning trades. You can put multiple currency pairs on your trading platform that share a common currency. As a U.S. citizen and knowing that the USD has long driven price movement in forex, I will routinely analyze price movement trajectory across four major pairs: EUR/USD, GBP/USD, USD/CHF, and USD/JPY.

What you should start to see is a pattern or parallel movement when there is a definitive causal effect related to the USD. This means, for instance, if you see EUR/USD and GBP/USD going up in value, and you also see USD/CHF and USD/JPY going down in value, the USD is weak. There are definitely times when you'll see lack of alignment in four pairs of this type. But, more routinely, you will see parallel movement. When you observe what looks like a common trend, you can then make one trade in each of the four pairs. This is a great way to profit in (at worst) two or three out of four currencies and end up with net profits.

Below is a sequence of screen shots showing this parallel behavior in currency pairs that all share a major currency that helps reveal causal effects. This is also how my trading platform is set up each day, so I highly recommend some nature of check and balance via multiple currencies. It definitely increases your winning percentages.

FOUNDATION TIME FRAMES (M15, M30, H1 – FOUR CURRENCY PAIRS)

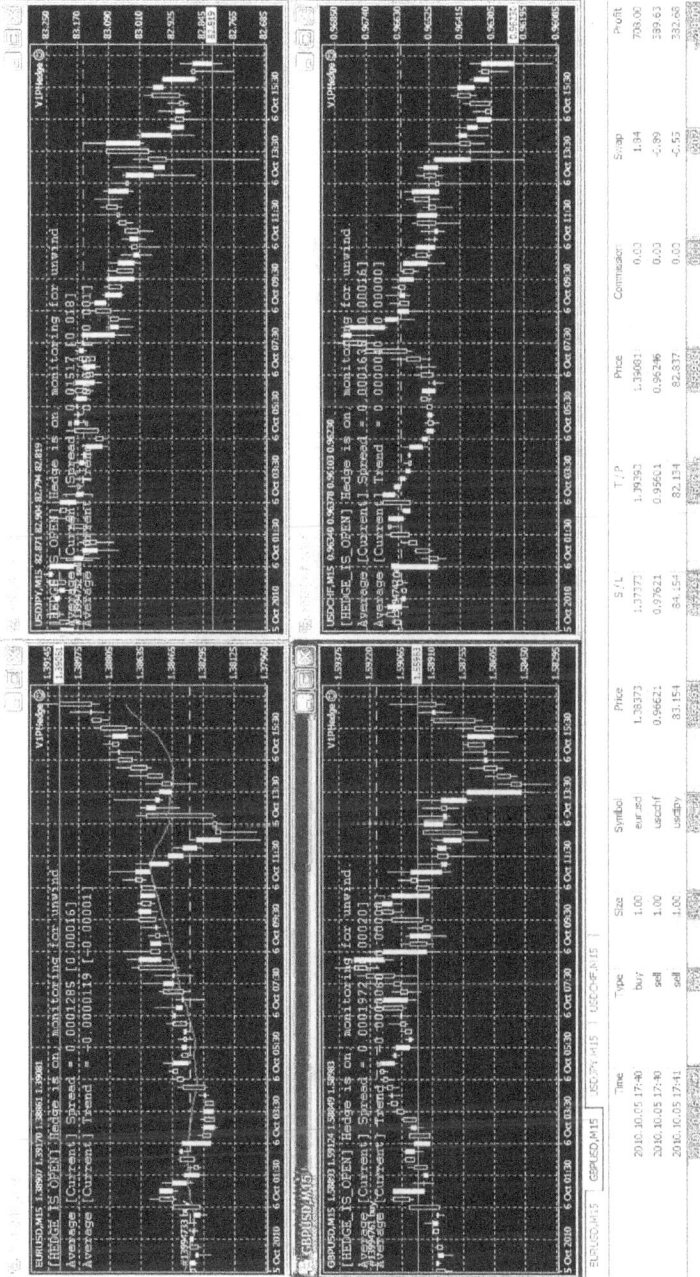

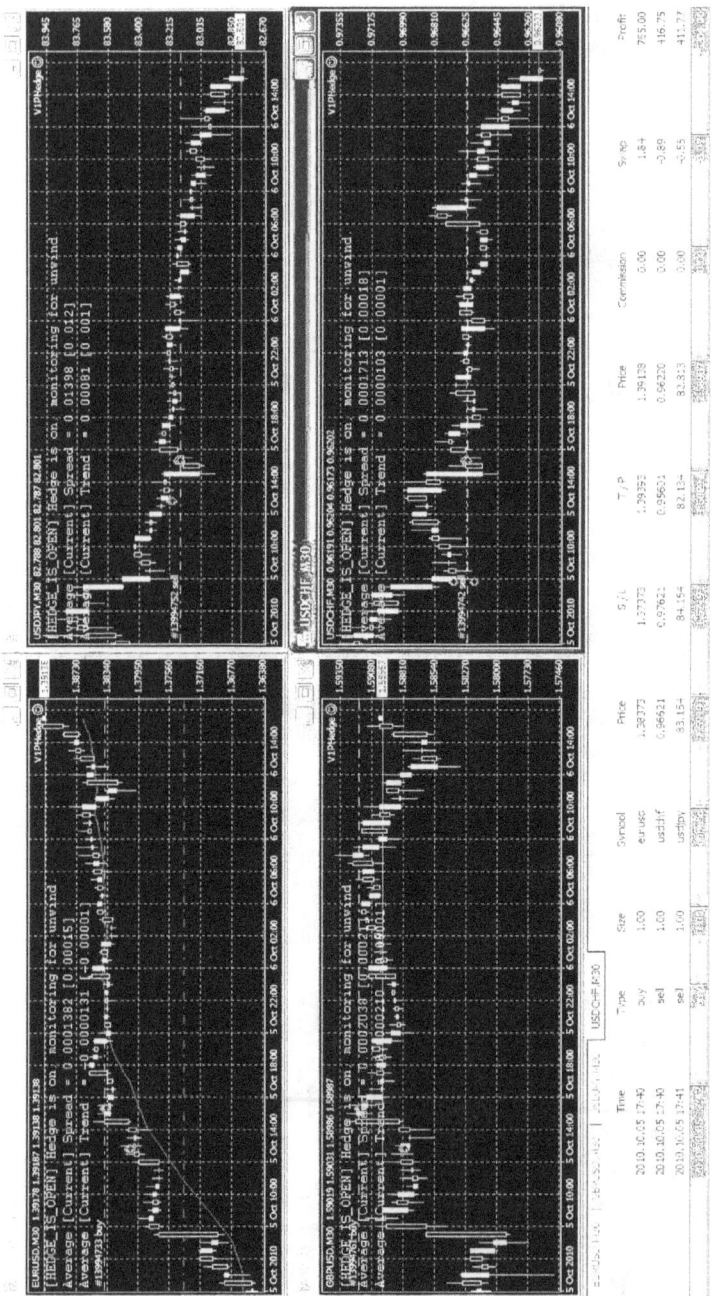

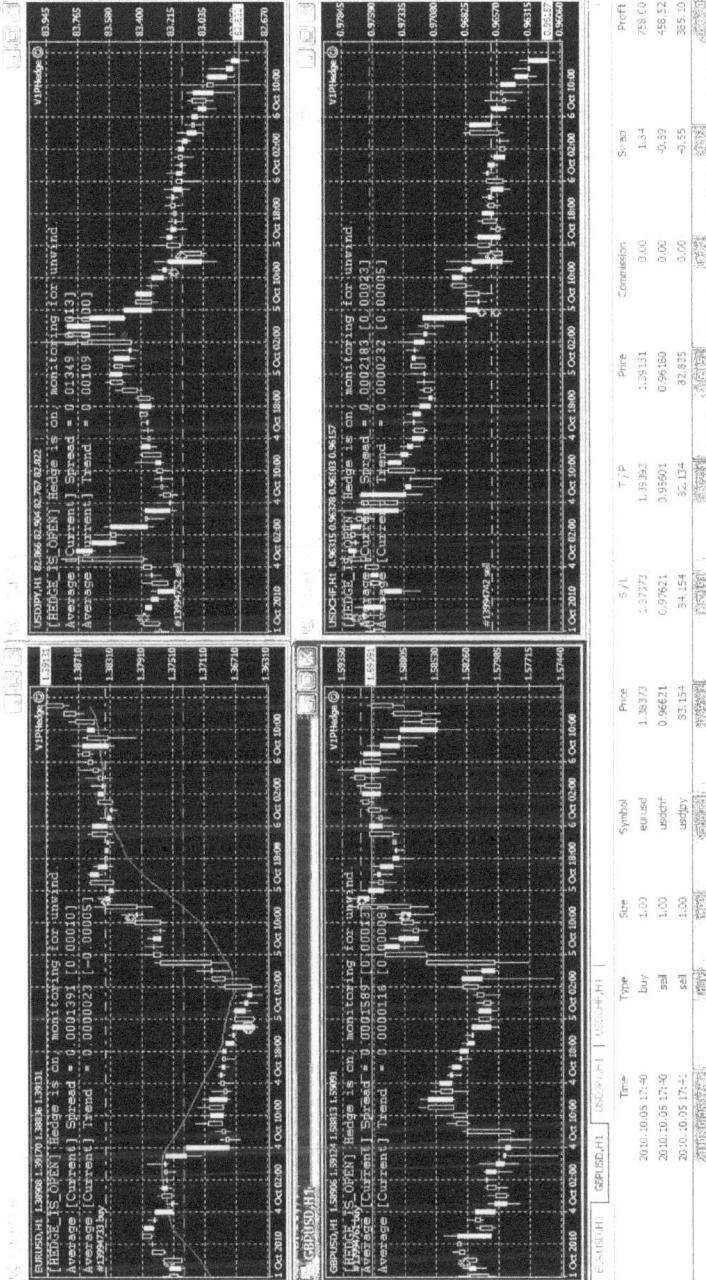

Time	Type	Size	Symbol	Price	S/L	T/P	Price	Commission	Swap	Profit
2010.10.05 17:40	buy	1.00	eurusd	1.38373	1.37373	1.39393	1.29131	0.00	1.34	758.00
2010.10.05 17:40	sell	1.00	usdchf	0.96621	0.97621	0.95601	0.96160	0.00	-0.39	458.52
2010.10.05 17:4:	sell	1.00	usdjpy	83.154	84.154	82.134	82.835	0.00	-0.55	385.10

You can see from the above time frames that we have price movement alignment with both EUR/USD and GBP/USD going up (increasing value of EUR and GBP/decreasing value of USD), and coordinate downward price movement with both USD/JPY and USD/CHF (decreasing value of USD/increasing value of JPY and CHF). So, we trade all four and, in this case, end up with profits on three of four based upon time of entry with each trade.

STRENGTH INDICATOR TIME FRAMES (H4, Daily, Weekly, Monthly)

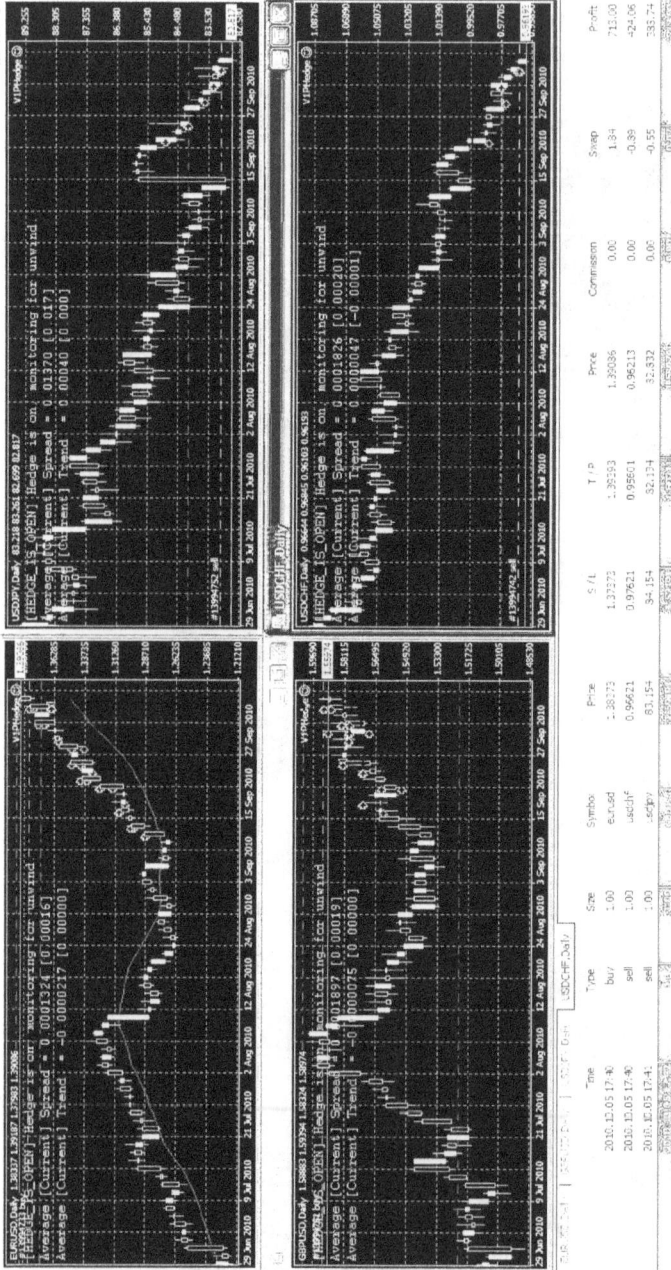

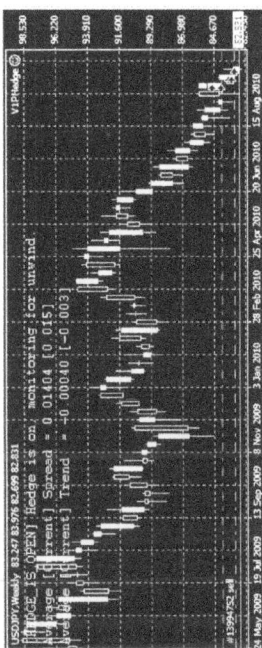

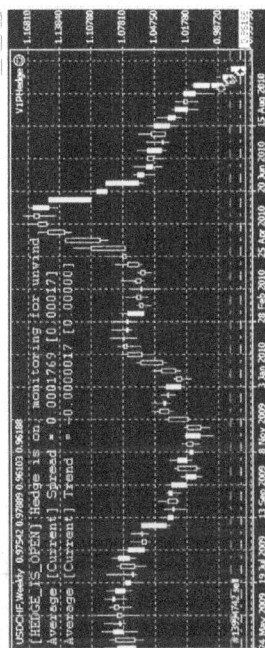

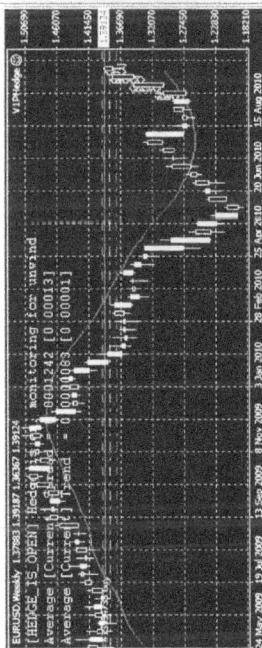

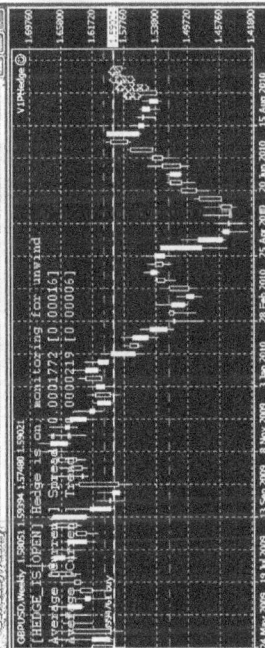

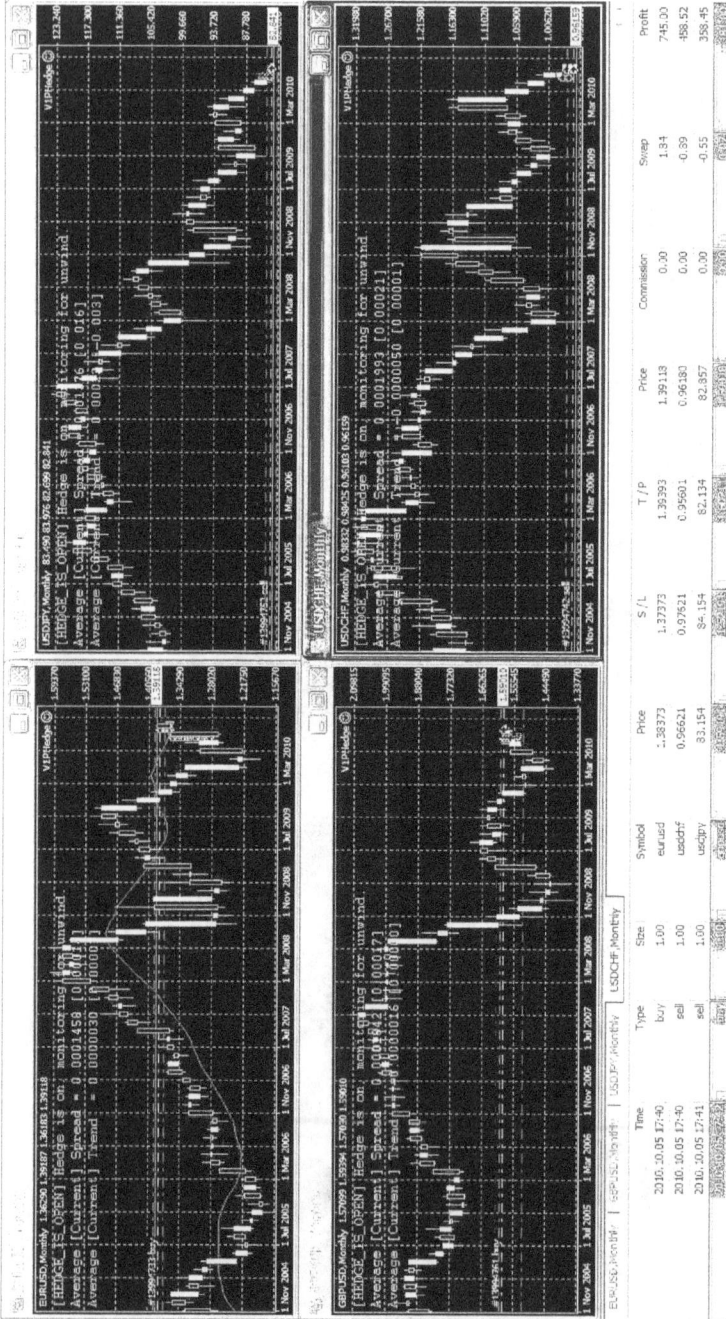

As you get into forex trading professionally, it's almost impossible for me to emphasize how important it will be to incorporate the above simple strategy with either USD or another shared currency like AUD, CHF, EUR, or JPY. Wisely trading multiple currency pairs which share a major currency such as USD, and thus reveal shared trajectory velocity resulting from common causal effects (or lack thereof), can be essential to the decisions that lead you to consistently profitable trading days.

Equally important, you will be able to protect yourself by diversification of your trades. With the above four pairs, for instance, I'd have lost money trading only the GBP/USD. Instead, by trading all four pairs, we ended up with a strong net profit.

As well, with real time data streaming in for an entire set of four pairs, and each sharing a cornerstone influence like USD currency, the entire trading day is more relaxed. Small retraces on one currency or another at different points in time become less of a concern since they are typically not reflected in all four pairs at the same time. And if you do see the same retrace happening at the same time in all four pairs, well, that tells you something important. Do you see the value in the above trading strategy?

The above example is how you trade forex profitably on a consistent basis with the Trajectory Forex methodology.

9

Confidence

There's an old saying in gambling that "scared money never wins". The phrase actually didn't originate with gamblers. It goes back to the 1940's in New York City when it was originally used to describe investors on Wall Street who would panic at the slightest indication of trouble. It applies to forex traders today, including those using the Trajectory Forex methodology. You can't win if you are trading money that you're afraid to lose.

This is a harsh reality you have to face when you make the decision to trade forex, but there are few things more true. If you can't afford to lose the money you're investing, then you shouldn't be investing. There's risk involved, and if your only focus is on the fact that you must make profits, then you'll likely lose.

I've heard a lot of successful traders tell me how they truly felt comfortable in forex only after they reached a point where it seemed more like a game than investing money. Earning pips became more like winning points in a game. They stopped thinking about it as winning or losing cash, and started looking at it as a challenge to beat the system.

That's a little part of what I was doing in the one example in an earlier set of charts where I advised you not to trade an observed retrace, yet I had a trade sitting there on the charts that went 100% against the advice I was giving you. I was perhaps overconfident. I was definitely breaking my own Max Loss Rule. But, I was also making a calm, confident, logical calculation of statistical probability that I could ride out that big retrace...and I won. Now, I know this contradicts a lot of what I've said up to this point, but this book is intended to get you started. With that in mind, perhaps the best way I can explain is to offer that the trading decisions you make four or five years into using this Trajectory methodology will evolve significantly compared to what you do the next couple months.

The simple fact is that I would have hated to lose in that instance, but I was not afraid to lose. I made a calculated decision. Not a guess. Not a prediction. Not a hope or a wish. It was a thoughtful decision based on the information I had to determine probabilities via the Trajectory methodology. I also had no fear of losing.

Even though I don't recommend taking such risks as riding out such a major retrace, the bigger point is that you cannot succeed if you have a fear of losing. It's perfectly normal and healthy to hate losing. It is fatal to fear losing.

People routinely talk about risk tolerance relative to investing, but the psychology involved in this emotional dynamic is a more complex consideration. A lot of people will take crazy risks. Just walk into any casino and observe the countless people gambling against long odds with money they truly cannot afford to lose. Yet, they KNOW the odds are remote that they'll win! Never become immune to the possibility of losing. HATE losing!

Risk tolerance, or the willingness to just throw your money away, is not a measure of the stuff needed psychologically to win trading forex.

This is about confidence. This is about zero fear. This is about the attitude that you can make trades and, win or lose; it's all okay because you do not fear losing. The paradox is that when you reach this place emotionally, you start winning a disgustingly high percentage of your trades. It's when you are truly liberated by calm and confidence that you suddenly tear up the market (provided you're utilizing the proper trading methodologies).

I dedicated this little chapter in the book to confidence because it is an essential key to success. It's an unfortunate reality, because the people who need this system most are the people who really "need" to make money in order to change their lives.

I have witnessed people dramatically change their fortunes via this system. I've trained people to win with Trajectory Forex when they were actually out of work and living off dwindling savings. I've trained people to win when they only had a couple hours a day to practice because they were working day and night jobs to pay the bills. I helped one woman with several kids, no husband, and only a night job as a cashier to completely change her life. She is now wealthy and trades professionally at her leisure. That one person's success story was enough to prompt the writing of this book and make me feel more pride than perhaps any other accomplishment in my professional trading life.

What I also observed about these people, who rose from near poverty to riches in forex, is that they did it through hard work and diligence. They were not impatient. They were not desperate despite their financial challenges. They were not quick to become angry and start forcing trades based on emotion. They seemingly had no fear and possessed a strong measure of serenity, calm and analytical confidence.

I can't explain it, but that's what I observed as I watched some of these people get into the Trajectory methodology and then invest with their own small amounts of money saved through hard work... money they actually could not afford to lose and acting against every piece of good, conventional advice one gives to a new trader. Yet, they made trades, won profits, and seemed immune to the pressure as they built a long track record of consistent winning and achieved financial independence.

I'm not selling you on this book or the Trajectory methodology. You've already bought the book, and I hope you've already clearly seen how Trajectory works.

I simply want to express that I don't know how to advise anyone on how to achieve this essential state of mental calm and confidence.

I just know that it's critical to your success. It causes me to think of some of the great religious leaders in our world or renowned philosophers who have that inner peace which comes from some higher power.

Perhaps these people whom I observed as they achieved success with Trajectory somehow "knew" they were destined for better things. Perhaps they were simply at a point in life where they felt there was nothing else left to lose, so they just let go emotionally and did it. Again, I can't explain the state of mind, but I know it is a vital asset. You will not succeed if you trade with skepticism or fear. Perhaps we can conclude that people may not succeed at anything in life if they approach it with skepticism and fear. Maybe that is the simple lesson here.

I have observed the focused peace of mind that wins. I have also seen people fail due to their tempers and frustrations, or unreasonably high and immediate financial goals, or get rich quick obsessions. The visibly greedy and openly desperate all seem to lose. The impatient seem destined to fail because they force trades. They perpetuate false hopes and see trends where they really don't exist. They talk themselves into tossing aside the logic of the Max Loss Rule. They ignore the warnings of sideways price movement.

These types of emotional traders might as well take that anger and frustration into a casino and throw their money on a craps table. You can't consistently win trades in forex or any market with the highly analytical Trajectory methodology if you are driven by high emotions.

Calm. Confidence. Positive attitude. These are shared characteristics of the people I've observed winning on a consistent basis over the past several years.

Does that make sense?

I hope so, because I will encourage you to delay trading forex (or any other market) unless and until you have that peace of mind and confidence. It's all about knowing you will win long before you've actually won.

You must also incorporate calm, logical money management

and do it all with the confident knowledge that somehow, you will win profits.

It's equally important to remember that this is a lifetime skill. You only have to learn the Trajectory Forex methodology one time, and then you should enjoy a lifetime of successful professional trading. So it's critical to be patient and diligent. Persistence is mandatory. You must be willing to fail and come back undeterred. You must be willing to make mistakes, and sometimes costly mistakes, but then come back to earn profits with a smile the next day.

You are inevitably going to screw up along the way. It is okay and part of the process even after you've been trading for years. Stay calm. Pretend you are sitting on your back porch (or actually sit on your back porch or deck with a wireless connection), and relax. You will not profit if you jump from one moment of panic to another. You must trust the logic of this data-based methodology, and live with confidence that success, for you, is the inevitable future.

SMALL ACCOUNT GROWS IN A MONTH

Price	Swap	Profit
5.9086	5.92	-323.26
1.65190	-16.80	91.00
1.65150	-16.80	146.00
1.9169	30.55	17.18
1.9169	30.55	17.18
1.9169	30.55	17.18
1.9156	30.55	34.40
1.46660	0.00	336.00
1.46664	0.00	160.00
1.46660	0.00	128.00
1.46658	0.00	16.00
1.46658	0.00	16.00
1.46658	0.00	16.00
1.46658	0.00	16.00
1.46658	0.00	16.00
1.46658	0.00	128.00
1.46777	0.00	864.00
1.46777	0.00	864.00
1.46777	0.00	864.00
1.46777	0.00	864.00
1.46777	0.00	864.00
1.46777	0.00	864.00
1.46777	0.00	864.00
1.46777	0.00	864.00
1.46777	0.00	864.00
1.46777	0.00	864.00
1.46777	0.00	824.00
1.46500	0.00	904.00
1.46500	0.00	1 048.00
1.46500	0.00	1 224.00
1.46500	0.00	1 232.00
1.46500	0.00	792.00
1.47103	0.00	2 048.00
1.47072	0.00	1 712.00
1.47044	0.00	1 456.00
1.47051	0.00	1 288.00
1.47047	0.00	1 216.00
1.47050	0.00	1 296.00
		81 189.25

Here Is The Daily Routine I Recommend

a. Start your morning by scanning through every currency pair for possible trends. Start with low spread pairs and work your way through the entire board. This process involves initially just looking over the three Foundation Time Frames (M15, M30 and H1). You should look through the entire population of currency pairs and jot down the ones where you may find a trend. Then go back and look into those pairs deeper.

b. If you have a doubt, there is no doubt. Do not trade when you tell yourself, "Well, it kind of looks like a trending trajectory so let me take a shot." No. Trust yourself. Trust your ability to identify trends. Trade only when you are saying to yourself, "Cool. Look at this!"

c. When you spot a possible price movement trend in the Foundation Time Frames (M15, M30 and H1), you will come back and look for alignment and velocity in this same trajectory in the Strength Indicator Time Frames (H4, Daily, Weekly, and Monthly).

d. If you only see alignment with steady velocity in the Foundation M15 through H1 time frames, then you may not NEED to see perfect alignment and constant velocity in the Strength Indicator Time Frames (H4, Daily, Weekly, and Monthly). This is common and it can still be a great opportunity for short term profit taking.

e. In the above scenario, you will next check the Short Term Trading Time Frames (M1 and M5) for alignment and velocity in the trend trajectory you see in the Foundation Time Frames. If you see the currency STILL moving the same direction in both short term time frames with no prolonged sideways movement (no uncertainty), enter your buy or sell trade and see if you can capture some profits!

f. Follow your rule for maximum loss if the trend moves against you X pips (whatever your pre-determined number is or a higher number "if" the profits have added up to the point where you can still come out with a net profit even with a bigger loss – this part is totally up to you). Bottom line: Stick to your Maximum Loss Rule unless there are exceptional circumstances! VERY exceptional.

g. When the trend ultimately ends, retraces beyond your Max Loss Rule, or stalls and goes sideways, close your trade win or lose. Then give the currency another half hour to an hour and see if it resumes the same trend. Or, if you don't have time to sit in front of your computer, just call it a day. If you picked intelligently, you ended with a net profit.

h. Key Things To Remember During This Ritual Process:

- Jot down any pair that is "close" to a trend on first scan
- Check "possible" trending pairs after 20 – 30 minutes
- Check "possible" trending pairs after a couple hours, 6 hours, 12 hours, 24 hours
- Consider putting a trade in place with stop and limit if you do not have time to stay in front of your computer, or put in a trailing stop
- Jot down currency pairs with only long term support for a particular trajectory in Strength Indicator Time Frames, then watch each morning for movement in that same direction when scanning the Foundation Time Frames. This is a quick way to spot big profit opportunities. It's how I found the Perfect Storm scenario noted earlier in this book.

i. After any extended session of profit taking, take a break of at least 15 minutes to an hour or consider calling it a day. This is not a mandatory part of my Trajectory Forex system, but it is an observation based on my own experience and what I've heard from other traders as being a wise thing to do. After a substantial win or sequence of winning trades, we tend to start thinking it's a "good day" or you're "on a roll". There is no such thing as a good day or being on a roll. There is only data and the intelligent, logical decisions you make based on that data. Never allow yourself to start looking for trends just because you've had a good day spotting one or two. Indeed, stopping while you're ahead is a good rule. Exactly when that is for you as an individual is impossible for me to say. I believe we all have to experience a few hard days where things go from good to bad before we begin to learn this lesson about ourselves. But you heard it here first. Don't press, don't hope, and don't wish trends into existence because you're feeling lucky. I don't believe in luck. Trading decisions made because you feel good about yourself are often unwise. The same is true about trading in a bad mood. That's another danger of emotions. Don't fall into that trap.

j. Perhaps the last thing I'll note has little to do with the system. I believe we covered how Trajectory Forex works and the simple steps you should take to implement this methodology. What's important is that you now put it into practice. I don't know a better way to learn this process than by doing. It's like a golf swing. You can read about the grip. You can study golf swings on video. But you will never really learn how to hit a golf ball correctly until you swing an actual club at that little white ball at your feet. Anyone who's done it also knows you likely won't hit that ball well until you've practiced for a while. The same is true of Trajectory Forex. Learn by doing. Practice. Make trades in demo.

Always stay in the positive frame of mind that you are constantly improving, and set up a nice, relaxing place where you feel comfortable trading every day.

10

Common Mistakes

People who have learned Trajectory Forex often make some consistent mistakes when starting out. Here are just a few things you may likely foul up. In the ideal scenario, this should happen only in demo practice. In reality, you may end up losing a little money with some of these mistakes. Hopefully, they will not be too costly and you'll recover with a lesson learned.

1. Don't be too confident. I know that I just forced you to read an entire chapter about confidence. At the same time, don't let yourself get carried away with overconfidence. Be smart. Never arrogant. Always use money management basics. Lose small. Win big. Always trust the data. It never lies. Know that you'll know beyond doubt when you can break the rules.

2. Don't get greedy. Do not talk yourself into seeing trends when they are not really there in the data. Instead, force yourself to check and double check price movement trajectory and velocity in time frames to make sure you have truly identified a trend with momentum. You cannot "make" a trend or price movement trajectory appear out of wishful thinking. You can only identify Trajectory price movement that is actually happening in the market as it shows up in the streaming real time data.

3. Don't be stubborn. Never believe a trend trajectory has so much velocity that it MUST continue. Everything changes. Every trend comes to an end. Even the strongest of trends can reverse on you in a matter of seconds. ALWAYS trust and trade based on what the data tells you. But remember that causal effects can change everything in the brief seconds it takes for two planes to crash into twin towers or for one nation to invade another or for a nuclear power plant to explode somewhere in the world or for simple financial data to be released by a major government. Causal effects CAN and DO happen without expectation and with dramatic impact. Always watch the real time stream of data when you are exposed in a live trade. Do NOT leave a trade alone at your computer unless you have money management stops and limits in place.

4. Do not continue to trust Technical Analysis or interpretation of fundamental events. Neither Technical nor Fundamental analysis work. Period. Never mix technical indicators or real world events with this data-based Trajectory system. The nature of causal effects that drive prices one trajectory or another are irrelevant. We do not care precisely "why" a trend is happening. All we need to do is identify when a trend is taking place. We do not care whether or not a price movement may or may not cross some historical or psychological barrier seen in past months or years. We do not care if a technical chart pattern emerges, because these are all based on historical observations and history does not predict the future. Trust only real time data. Period. Trade In The Now.

5. Don't get caught without enough free margin. Keep about half your account as free margin as a general principle, but also talk to your broker relative to their rules in this regard. For those who are new to forex, always keep enough free margin in your account to avoid a margin call. As a rule, you should keep about half or more of your account equity available as free margin until you achieve about $10,000 total account equity. Above that point, $5000 in free margin "should" be enough up through $15,000 account equity (which is the maximum we recommend leaving on account with any broker). It is always a good idea to talk to your broker and ask about their

individual margin requirements. Your broker sets their own rules, and it seems like these rules are constantly changing, so always consult your broker about margin requirements.

6. Do not violate your Maximum Loss Rule. It is only in rare instances that you will allow a trend to move against you beyond your maximum loss limit. If you have determined that you will lose only 5 pips if a trade goes against you, then always exit the trade when you hit a 5 pip loss. The exception is when you've earned significantly more profits than your Maximum Loss amount. In these cases, you can allow yourself to lose a third to half the profits in order to try and ride out a small retrace in what is clearly a strong and correctly identified trend trajectory.

7. Your actions determine your success or failure. I have never had anyone tell me that this system "does not work". What I have heard from a few traders who never actually bothered to implement the system is that they "don't understand" or that it's "too complicated" or this is "too subjective". These comments always come from people who later admit that they didn't actually practice for a couple weeks in demo or, in some cases, never read the entire book. Or they never bothered to study the charts as I advise. Trajectory Forex is truly not a "subjective" trend identification methodology. It is a data based system that utilizes real time, streaming information to calculate price movement trajectory and determine the statistical probability that the movement will continue in the same direction. Since this is data based, and both variables we analyze in real time are known to be 100% true at all times, Trajectory Forex is purely analytical...not subjective. It definitely involves an element of interpretation relative to the data, but the price movement trajectory and velocity are constantly visible in the data. Trajectory Forex is about making qualitative decisions based on exact and true quantitative data.

8. Don't be a wishful thinker. Perhaps the biggest single mistake made is when new traders attempt to subjectively use wishful thinking to believe they see a price movement trend trajectory. New traders often end up making this methodology of data analysis subjective in order to impatiently envision trading opportunities that aren't actu-

ally there. If you rely only on the data, you should consistently win trades. But you will also identify more situations where a trend is not present versus legitimate profit taking opportunities. So conservative thinking and patient diligence are essential. Avoid letting emotions, hopes, and dreams of overnight riches dictate your thinking, and you should succeed.

9. Don't be lazy and believe that reading this book is going to lead to instant wealth. No one is going to give you money just because you bought this book about the Trajectory Forex system. You are not "entitled" to profits. You must earn your profits through the hard work of studying, practicing and mastering this system. One way I explain how hard it is to earn profits is by pointing out that money is not manufactured out of thin air. If you earn one dollar by trading forex, what's really happened is that you took one dollar out of another trader's pocket. That's the constant battle waged in every marketplace where trading takes place.

Whether it's forex or conventional stocks on a major exchange, if there is a winner who earns profits then there is a coordinate opponent who's lost money. And no one gives up their cash easily. So, when you earn profits, you will "earn" them. It's work. Never underestimate the measure of work required to achieve true wealth. Just because you've discovered a proven methodology in this book for winning trades does not mean YOU will win trades. It means you have the opportunity to win trades "if" you learn this system and "if" you can execute it with discipline and intelligence over a long period of time.

You can read a great book about a proven weight loss diet, but it will not make you thin. Are you ready to work at making money?

11

Just Have Fun

Trajectory Forex is not a game. It's serious. It's work. It takes hard work to master. Yet, you really should have fun when you're trading forex. If you can make it fun, and still appreciate the hard work involved, then you have the essential ingredients for long term success.

How many things in life do you do every day that you absolutely do not enjoy? Sadly, a lot of people will quickly say they don't enjoy their jobs. The truth is that people typically find some aspect of their work to enjoy, even if it's just a friend or two with whom they can talk during breaks or at lunch. Being able to enjoy yourself through the many daily hours of what is fundamentally "work" is essential. The more fun you have, then the more likely you will work harder.

Trajectory Forex has been documented to consistently identify profitable price movement trends since 2006. If you fail to make profits on a consistent basis, you should look in the mirror because it's likely you who's missed something. Or perhaps you're just not enjoying the process of trading forex. Or perhaps you put too much pressure on yourself to make money quickly. Or maybe it's just too intense or pressurized for you to make calm, logical decisions. Or maybe you really can't afford to suffer even a small loss and every decision is based on fear of failure.

Be aware that the thinking process requires an open, logical mind. You can't make decisions if you're in something of a panic or intensely worried about every single move you're about to make.

Trust the data. Don't give up if you screw up. Realize that no one on Earth can predict the future. All I've done here is open your eyes to the truth, value and merit of statistical probability. All I've done is reveal how to most simply and accurately calculate the trajectory and velocity of price movement (like a virtual object in motion) with the two and only two pieces of 100% true data we have in forex: price movement and time.

Still, even with the power of this data, statistical probability is all we have to identify trend momentum in forex or any other endeavor in the known universe. Will the sun rise tomorrow morning? I believe it will, but that's based on statistical probability. An asteroid could hit Earth tonight, and we might never see another sunrise. Will a car moving 100 mph north over the past hour continue moving north for another 50 feet over the next few seconds? Statistical probability says yes, but there could also be a concrete wall hidden from view just 20 feet ahead.

Statistical probability of price movement trending is indeed about "probability"…not guarantees. No matter what the data shows you, there is no sure thing.

The best you can do is put the odds in your favor via objective, empirical, real time data analysis. You can stack the deck in your favor by making decisions based on such strong statistical probabilities. You can consistently refuse to lose big when you miss, and always capture maximum profits when you hit winners. This is how you will achieve increasingly large net profits on a regular basis.

Most importantly, you must enjoy the process. If you enjoy the process of analyzing the data to win trades, then you'll do it more often and you'll get better.

That's all there is to Trajectory Forex. Just remember to practice in a free demo account before you trade a single dollar of cash. Prove to yourself that you know how to win trades in demo. Then open a cash account and go live.

It is impossible for me to show you every combination of price movements in every time frame. There are truly infinite combinations of price movement patterns you will see over time. You must undertake the task of identifying the trajectory price movements that are trending and then calculating their relative velocity through evaluating different time frames.

While there are variations far too diverse and extensive to show you as examples, what you should be able to identify right this moment are the extreme examples of price movement with a clear trajectory and strong velocity, which identifies high statistical probability of continued momentum and profit opportunity. Or, equally important, you should be able to identify a price movement trajectory that is not trending or has little to no trustworthy velocity. Through practice, you will further refine your ability to identify the relative merits of trending that exist in between the extremes.

Always remember that being able to identify the absence of a trending trajectory is just as important as finding a winning trend.

Identification of those situations where there is NOT a trend or strong price movement trajectory is very likely the best way for you to start implementing Trajectory Forex. Start to identify scenarios where you believe there is a profit taking trend. Then, challenge yourself. Look for weaknesses in the trend you "think" you've identified. After you make a decision that it looks like a trend, but you doubt it, observe price movement to see if you were right. This is yet another way to practice the system and further develop your trend identification skills. It will also be valuable in terms of helping you avoid losses! Again, identifying those instances where there is NOT a trend is a valuable skill.

Identification of threats to ongoing price movement trajectory will ultimately help you avoid costly mistakes, so this is a skill well worth practice. Look for traps and situations where you may see what looks like a trend in a few key time frames, but really turns out to be misleading interpretation of price movement trajectory and velocity.

Since there are typically more cases of currencies not legitimately trending at any given point in time, you will likely have more success initially in identifying negative situations where there is less statistical probability of opportunity to make a profit versus trying to immediately identify a true trend.

Ultimately, your individual practice and dedication to continuously improve at the processes outlined in this book will lead you to profits in forex or any other market where you choose to implement Trajectory price movement trend identification.

Just imagine. What if you can actually do everything discussed in this book? Wouldn't it be fun to beat the system? Wouldn't it be amazing to achieve every financial goal you've imagined by practicing Trajectory and then winning at forex?

It's up to you! The world of forex and the future world in which you live are now in your hands. Embrace and enjoy this opportunity. Have fun. In the end, this book has merely given you a tool. What you build with it depends on your attitude and dedication to win.

Go for it!

NO WARRANTY DISCLAIMER AND FOREX RISK
DISCLOSURE

THIS IS AN INVESTMENT PRODUCT THAT IS NOT GUARANTEED TO PRODUCE RESULTS. RESULTS VARY AS WITH ANY INVESTMENT. THIS SYSTEM CANNOT BE GUARANTEED TO PRODUCE RESULTS FOR YOU. ANY MONEY YOU INVEST IS AT RISK AND CAN BE LOST. THE AUTHORS OF THIS TRAJECTORY SYSTEM CANNOT GUARANTEE ANY NATURE OF PERFORMANCE OR PROFIT. INVESTMENT PRODUCTS ARE INHERENTLY RISKY AND ANY MONEY YOU INVEST IS SOLELY AT YOUR OWN RISK. THE AUTHORS ACCEPT NO RESPONSIBILITY NOR CAN BE HELD LIABLE FOR YOUR ACTIONS BASED UPON ANY INFORMATION CONTAINED HEREIN. THE VALUE OF INVESTMENTS MAY GO UP OR DOWN DUE TO VARIOUS FACTORS, INCLUDING BUT NOT LIMITED TO CHANGES IN FOREIGN EXCHANGE RATES, AND INVESTORS MAY NOT GET BACK AMOUNT(S) INVESTED. THE AUTHOR AND ALL AFFILIATES HEREBY DISCLAIM ANY RESPONSIBILITY AND LIABILITY WHATSOEVER IN THIS RESPECT. DUE TO HIGH LEVERAGE, YOU ARE SUBJECT TO MARGIN CALLS AND SUB-STANTIAL LOSSES. THE TRAJECTORY SYSTEM IS DESIGNED TO GIVE YOU A STATISTICAL ADVANTAGE IN IDENTIFYING TRENDS, BUT THERE IS NO GUARANTEE YOU WILL EFFECTIVELY IMPLEMENT THIS SYSTEM FOR PROFIT. PERFORMANCE WILL VARY DEPENDING UPON YOUR OWN PERFORMANCE. THE AUTHORS CANNOT, ARE NOT AND WILL NOT BE RESPONSIBLE FOR LOSSES YOU SUFFER. THE INVESTOR TAKES FULL

RESPONSIBILITY FOR THEIR OWN ACTIONS. THE AUTHORS ARE NOT AFFILIATED WITH ANY BROKER NOR RESPONSIBLE FOR CHANGES IN REGULATIONS OR LAWS THAT APPLY TO YOU. FOREX IS INHERENTLY RISKY. YOU SHOULD NEVER INVEST MONEY YOU CANNOT AFFORD TO LOSE. THERE IS NO WARRANTY OR GUARANTEE OF PERFORMANCE WITH THIS FINANCIAL INVESTMENT PRODUCT. THERE IS NO INHERENT VALUE CLAIMED OR ASSERTED IN THE CONTENTS OF THIS SYSTEM, THIS DOCUMENT OR THE WEBSITE ASSOCIATED WITH THIS DOCU-MENT OR THE TRAJECTORY SYSTEM. THE AUTHORS CANNOT ASSUME LIABILITY FOR ANY FINANCIAL LOSSES. NEITHER THE AUTHOR NOR ANYONE ASSOCIATED WITH THE TRAJECTORY SYSTEM ARE LICENSED PROFESSIONAL BUSINESS COUNSELORS OR FINANCIAL ADVISORS.

NO GUARANTEE IS MADE AS TO THE AMOUNT OF MONEY YOU MAY PROFIT OR LOSE BY EMPLOYING THE STRATEGIES STATED IN THIS BOOK. EMPLOY ALL IDEAS AT YOUR OWN RISK. THE TRAJECTORY SYS-TEM IS SOLD WITH THE UNDERSTANDING THAT NEITHER THE AUTHOR NOR THE PUBLISHER IS ENGAGED IN RENDERING PROFESSIONAL OR INVESTMENT SERVICES. IF PROFESSIONAL ADVICE OR OTHER EXPERT ASSISTANCE IS REQUIRED, THE SERVICES OF A COMPETENT PROFES-SIONAL PERSON SHOULD BE SOUGHT. THE AUTHOR AND ALL PARTIES ASSOCIATED WITH THE TRAJECTORY SYSTEM ARE NOT LICENSED FI-NANCIAL ADVISORS, REGISTERED INVESTMENT ADVISORS OR REG-ISTERED BROKERS OR DEALERS. WE DO NOT PROVIDE INVESTMENT OR FINANCIAL ADVICE OR MAKE INVESTMENT RECOMMENDATIONS. THE INFORMATION, LINKS AND RESOURCES HEREIN MAY LINK YOU TO THE USE OF INVESTING STRATEGIES, BUT THIS IS NOT INVESTMENT, FINANCIAL OR OTHER ADVICE. NOTHING CONTAINED IN THIS BOOK OR ANY ASSOCIATED OR SUBSEQUENT COMMUNICATIONS OR FILES TRANSMITTED CONSTITUTES A SOLICITATION, RECOMMENDATION, PROMOTION, ENDORSEMENT OR OFFER TO BUY OR SELL BY THE AU-THOR OR PUBLISHER ANY OF THE PROVIDED RESOURCES, NOR OF ANY PARTICULAR CURRENCY, SECURITY, MUTUAL FUND, TRANSACTION OR INVESTMENT. THIS DOCUMENT DOES NOT HAVE INHERENT OR IM-PLIED VALUE OF ANY NATURE. PAST OR SIMULATED PERFORMANCE DOES NOT GUARANTEE FUTURE RESULTS. ONLY YOU ARE LIABLE

FOR YOUR INVESTMENT AND TRADING DECISIONS AND YOU AGREE TO HOLD THE AUTHOR HARMLESS AND WITHOUT LIABILITY FROM YOUR INVESTMENT DECISIONS. THERE ARE NO IMPLIED OR EXPRESS WARRANTIES OF MERCHANTABILITY OR FITNESS FOR A PARTICULAR PURPOSE. PLEASE USE YOUR DUE DILIGENCE AND GOVERN YOURSELF ACCORDINGLY. EVERY EFFORT HAS BEEN MADE TO ENSURE THAT AC-CURATE REPRESENTATION OF THESE PRODUCTS AND SERVICES AND THEIR POTENTIAL FOR INCOME. EARNING AND INCOME STATEMENTS ARE ESTIMATES OF WHAT WE THINK YOU CAN POSSIBLY EARN. THERE IS NO GUARANTEE THAT YOU WILL MAKE THESE AMOUNTS OF IN-COME AND YOU ACCEPT THE RISK THAT THE EARNINGS AND INCOME STATEMENTS DIFFER BY INDIVIDUAL. THERE ARE NO GUARANTEES CONCERNING THE LEVEL OF SUCCESS YOU MAY EXPERIENCE. THE EXAMPLES USED ARE NOT INTENDED TO REPRESENT OR GUARANTEE THAT ANYONE WILL ACHIEVE THE SAME OR SIMILAR RESULTS. EACH INDIVIDUAL'S SUCCESS DEPENDS ON HIS OR HER BACKGROUND, DED-ICATION, DESIRE AND MOTIVATION. THERE IS NO ASSURANCE THAT EXAMPLES OF PAST EARNINGS CAN BE DUPLICATED IN THE FUTURE. THERE ARE UNKNOWN RISKS IN BUSINESS, FOREX, INVESTING IN GEN-ERAL AND ANY ACTIVITY ON THE INTERNET THAT WE CANNOT FORE-SEE WHICH CAN IMPACT RESULTS. WE ARE NOT RESPONSIBLE FOR YOUR ACTIONS. THE USE OF OUR INFORMATION, PRODUCTS AND SER-VICES SHOULD BE BASED ON YOUR OWN DUE DILIGENCE. YOU AGREE THAT THE AUTHOR AND ALL INDIVIDUALS AFFILIATED WITH THIS BOOK AND THE TRAJECTORY SYSTEM ARE NOT LIABLE FOR ANY FI-NANCIAL OR OTHER SUCCESS OR FAILURE THAT IS DIRECTLY OR INDI-RECTLY RELATED TO THE PURCHASE AND USE OF OUR INFORMATION, PRODUCTS AND SERVICES. PLEASE READ THIS CAREFULLY. IF YOU DON'T UNDERSTAND ANY OF THE INFORMATION PROVIDED IN THIS DISCLOSURE OR IF YOU HAVE ANY QUESTIONS, PLEASE CONTACT US. THE NATIONAL FUTURES ASSOCIATION (NFA) AND CFTC (COMMODITY FUTURES TRADING COMMISSION), THE REGULATORY AGENCIES FOR THE FOREX AND FUTURES MARKET IN THE UNITED STATES, REQUIRE THAT CUSTOMERS BE INFORMED ABOUT THE FOLLOWING POTENTIAL RISKS IN THE FOREX MARKET:

RISKS ASSOCIATED WITH FOREX AND TRADING

TRADING FOREIGN CURRENCIES IS A CHALLENGING AND PO-TENTIALLY PROFITABLE OPPORTUNITY FOR EDUCATED AND EXPERI-ENCED INVESTORS. HOWEVER, BEFORE DECIDING TO PARTICIPATE IN THE FOREX MARKET, YOU SHOULD CAREFULLY CONSIDER YOUR IN-VESTMENT OBJECTIVES, LEVEL OF EXPERIENCE AND RISK APPETITE. MOST IMPORTANTLY, DO NOT INVEST MONEY YOU CANNOT AFFORD TO LOSE.

THERE IS CONSIDERABLE EXPOSURE TO RISK IN ANY FOREIGN EXCHANGE TRANSACTION. ANY TRANSACTION INVOLVING CURREN-CIES INVOLVES RISKS INCLUDING, BUT NOT LIMITED TO, THE POTEN-TIAL FOR CHANGING POLITICAL AND/OR ECONOMIC CONDITIONS THAT MAY SUBSTANTIALLY AFFECT THE PRICE OR LIQUIDITY OF A CURRENCY.

MOREOVER, THE LEVERAGED NATURE OF FOREX TRADING MEANS THAT ANY MARKET MOVEMENT WILL HAVE AN EQUALLY PRO-PORTIONAL EFFECT ON YOUR DEPOSITED FUNDS. THIS MAY WORK AGAINST YOU AS WELL AS FOR YOU. THE POSSIBILITY EXISTS THAT YOU COULD SUSTAIN A TOTAL LOSS OF INITIAL MARGIN FUNDS AND BE REQUIRED TO DEPOSIT ADDITIONAL FUNDS TO MAINTAIN YOUR POSITION. IF YOU FAIL TO MEET ANY MARGIN CALL WITHIN THE TIME PRESCRIBED, YOUR POSITION WILL BE LIQUIDATED AND YOU WILL BE RESPONSIBLE FOR ANY RESULTING LOSSES. INVESTORS MAY LOWER THEIR EXPOSURE TO RISK BY EMPLOYING RISK-REDUCING STRATE-GIES SUCH AS 'STOP-LOSS' OR 'LIMIT' ORDERS.

THERE ARE ALSO RISKS ASSOCIATED WITH UTILIZING AN INTER-NET-BASED DEAL EXECUTION SOFTWARE APPLICATION INCLUDING, BUT NOT LIMITED TO THE FAILURE OF HARDWARE AND SOFTWARE.

TRADING FOREIGN EXCHANGE ON MARGIN CARRIES A HIGH LEVEL OF RISK, AND MAY NOT BE SUITABLE FOR ALL INVESTORS. THE HIGH DEGREE OF LEVERAGE CAN WORK AGAINST YOU AS WELL AS FOR YOU. BEFORE DECIDING TO INVEST IN FOREIGN EXCHANGE YOU SHOULD CAREFULLY CONSIDER YOUR INVESTMENT OBJECTIVES, LEVEL OF EXPERIENCE, AND RISK APPETITE. THE POSSIBILITY EXISTS THAT YOU COULD SUSTAIN A LOSS OF SOME OR ALL OF YOUR INITIAL

INVESTMENT AND THEREFORE YOU SHOULD NOT INVEST MONEY THAT YOU CANNOT AFFORD TO LOSE. YOU SHOULD BE AWARE OF ALL THE RISKS ASSOCIATED WITH FOREIGN EXCHANGE TRADING, AND SEEK ADVICE FROM AN INDEPENDENT FINANCIAL ADVISOR IF YOU HAVE ANY DOUBTS.

PROFIT AND LOSS POTENTIAL

IN ANY MARKET WHERE A POTENTIAL FOR PROFIT EXISTS, THERE EXISTS ALSO A RISK OF LOSS. NONE OF THE INFORMATION IN THE TRAJECTORY SYSTEM NOR ANY INFORMATION OR EDUCATION PROVIDED TO THE CLIENT BY ANY MEANS ASSURES THAT THE CLIENT WILL MAKE MONEY IN THE FOREX MARKET. THE INFORMATION CONTAINED IN THIS DOCUMENT AND ON THIS WEBSITE DOES NOT CONSTITUTE INVESTMENT ADVICE. THE AUTHORS OF THIS CONTENT AND CREATORS OF THIS WEBSITE WILL NOT AND DO NOT ACCEPT LIABILITY FOR ANY LOSS OR DAMAGE, INCLUDING WITHOUT LIMITATION TO, ANY LOSS OF PROFIT, WHICH MAY ARISE DIRECTLY OR INDIRECTLY FROM USE OF OR RELIANCE ON SUCH INFORMATION.

BENEFITS AND RISKS OF LEVERAGE

EVEN THOUGH THE FOREX MARKET OFFERS TRADERS THE ABILITY TO USE A HIGH DEGREE OF LEVERAGE, TRADING WITH HIGH LEVERAGE MAY INCREASE THE LOSSES SUFFERED. PLEASE USE CAUTION WHEN USING LEVERAGE IN TRADING OR INVESTING.

HYPOTHETICAL PERFORMANCE OR BACK-TESTED RESULTS

HYPOTHETICAL PERFORMANCE RESULTS HAVE MANY INHERENT LIMITATIONS. NO REPRESENTATION IS BEING MADE THAT ANY ACCOUNT WILL OR IS LIKELY TO ACHIEVE PROFITS OR LOSSES SIMILAR TO THOSE INFERRED OR SHOWN. THERE ARE FREQUENTLY SHARP DIFFERENCES BETWEEN HYPOTHETICAL PERFORMANCE RESULTS AND THE ACTUAL RESULTS SUBSEQUENTLY ACHIEVED BY A PARTICULAR TRADING ACTIVITY. ONE OF THE LIMITATIONS OF HYPOTHETICAL PERFORMANCE RESULTS IS THEY ARE GENERALLY PREPARED WITH THE BENEFIT OF HINDSIGHT. IN ADDITION, HYPOTHETICAL TRADING DOES NOT INVOLVE FINANCIAL RISK AND NO HYPOTHETICAL TRADING RECORD CAN COMPLETELY ACCOUNT FOR THE IMPACT OF FINANCIAL RISK IN ACTUAL TRADING. THE ABILITY TO WITHSTAND LOSSES OR

ADHERE TO A PARTICULAR TRADING PROGRAM IN SPITE OF TRADING LOSSES ARE MATERIAL POINTS WHICH CAN ADVERSELY AFFECT ACTUAL TRADING RESULTS. THERE ARE MANY OTHER FACTORS RELATED TO THE MARKETS IN GENERAL OR TO THE IMPLEMENTATION OF A SPECIFIC TRADING PROGRAM WHICH CANNOT BE FULLY ACCOUNTED FOR IN THE PREPARATION OF HYPOTHETICAL PERFORMANCE RESULTS; ALL OF WHICH CAN ADVERSELY AFFECT ACTUAL TRADING RESULTS.

www.ingramcontent.com/pod-product-compliance
Lightning Source LLC
Chambersburg PA
CBHW071905200326
41519CB00016B/4512